Developing the Intelligent Young Footballer

By Mike Mair

Copyright © Mair Development Ltd 2021.

The right of Mike Mair to be identified as the author of this work has been asserted in accordance with the Copyright, Designs and Patents Act 1988.

All rights reserved. No part of this publication may be reproduced, stored in or transmitted into any retrieval system, in any form, or by any means (electronic, mechanical, photocopying, recording or otherwise) without the prior written permission of the publisher. Any person who does any unauthorised act in relation to this publication may be liable to criminal prosecution and civil claims for damages.

ISBN: 978-1-913012-53-3

Published in partnership with Riverside Publishing Solutions.

This book is dedicated to my family and friends

To my Dad, so much of who I am and what I am is a result of his influence.

To my Mum, for unwavering support in everything I did growing up.

To my wife, Sonia, my true companion, and for putting up with everything football.

To my sister Alison and brother-in-law Les, very special to me.

To my boys, Lewis and Daniel, and for creating and sharing special memories.

To all my friends, I am a lucky man.

Never above you, never below you, always by your side.

Cheers.

Contents

Read this book if...	viii
Foreword	x
Background and Introduction	xiv
Chapter 1: Why do you do it?	1
Chapter 2: Being a Real and Good Coach	7
Chapter 3: Have a Transparent Recruitment Policy	21
Chapter 4: Let the Game be the Teacher	33
Chapter 5: Be Interested in their Development	45
Chapter 6: Have a Clear Strategy and Vision for your Team	61
Chapter 7: How do you Measure Success and Development?	90
Chapter 8: Be a Good Communicator and an Even Better Listener	100
Chapter 9: Help your Players with Education and Game Progression (Beyond the Game)	114
Chapter 10: Influential and inspirational quotes	126
Chapter 11: Respected Coaches	131
Chapter 12: Feedback from Children	139
Chapter 13: Celebrating Learning with and From Children	147
Chapter 14: Continue to Develop Yourself	149

Read this book if...

- ✓ **You are starting out on this privileged and incredible journey of being a football coach and have the opportunity to influence, inspire, grow and develop the intelligent young footballer.**

- ✓ **You are in need of a 'pick me up', to challenge yourself to learn something new and improve and develop yourself as a coach and developer of young footballers.**

- ✓ **You want the permission to pause and reflect on what you already do. There are over 80 self-reflection questions in this book.**

- ✓ **You just want to read someone else's story, to look for inspiration, or maybe just to validate that what you do is right.**

- ✓ **You are interested in Leadership and People Development both in business and in a sporting context.**

"Football is fun and football is an educator of life skills"

Ian Gillan
Technical Director
Kedah FC

Foreword

This book has been written with the intent to share my amazing experiences and my learning in developing the intelligent young footballer. Throughout the book I will refer to young footballers or children, they are one and the same thing. In the context of this book they are Under 18 (U18) boys or girls.

Let me start by saying that I haven't always got it right, far from it, but I have had some incredible experiences and have some great memories.

Many people find personal challenges to motivate and engage themselves such as climbing Everest, walking The Great Wall of China, or running the London Marathon. Whatever it is, I admire and respect your choice. For me the whole experience of developing intelligent young footballers is a motivational and engaging experience to match.

In reading this book, you will not agree with everything I say, I don't expect you to, but if it challenges your thinking and approaches and gives you the time and permission to do so, then I will be pleased to have played that part. Alternatively, at some points you will have that aha moment where you think, that is how you do it. You have learned something new and with potential actions to take to develop yourself.

If this book challenges your thinking, then great. If this book validates your thinking, then that is equally good. Challenging yourself to learn something new and different, or validating that what you do is right is effective learning.

Throughout this book I will ask you a number of questions for your own personal self-reflection and development. Don't just read them, give yourself the time and permission to pause and consider and if you want, scribble down your answers.

In Coaching, if you ask the right questions, it inspires people to find their own solutions, and this is one of my intents, to influence and inspire and to act as a coach for you.

This book does not contain training drills, there are plenty of great books and sources of learning that you can find on that subject. My intent is more about my strategy, and approaches to interacting and engaging with children and their parents.

Whatever stage you are at, whether it is starting out with a new team, or part way through the journey and age groups of youth football or nearing the end of your time developing children before adult football… enjoy the read.

Reflect on what you do and recognise all that you do really well. It is important that you recognise that because at times it can be a lonely job. For most of you, you will be volunteers but there will still be massive expectations on you to do everything right first time.

If you identify an area that you could improve on, do it. Don't try, personally I think 'try' is a weak word. Do it. If there is no action, there will be no learning. There will be no learning, without action.

One thing I learned very early on in my journey was to always ask for feedback. I believe that if you surround yourself with feedback, you can only get better.

Personally, I haven't found a book that is a collective like this is intended. I have found plenty of nuggets and great learning along the way whether in other books or on the internet, but not in a collective. When discussing my plan with another respected coach he said, "I wish there was something like that around when I started". My book is my story that I feel compelled to share, and if in any way I can help you to help develop young children and young footballers then great.

There will be plenty of challenges along the way but above all, enjoy the experience of being a football coach and mentor. It ultimately is a pleasure and a privileged position that we are in to be able make a positive impact on people's lives.

"I think what probably says the most about how I feel about you is that I convinced Stefano to join you with Milton Colts (obviously before we found out

Foreword

we were moving). I did so because I have known you as a teacher with great preparation and discipline but also with tremendous patience and compassion. I couldn't imagine little Stefano in better hands. Those kids in the Milton Colts are lucky because they will be as good as they can be.

You have taught me a lot. I can never emulate your style, but I have learned a lot about how to approach a learning environment by watching you. Thanks for being a part of my life these last 13 years. I am much the richer for it."

**Antony Mattesich,
President and CEO at Ocular Therapeutix, Inc.**

Background and Introduction

So, why would you want to read a book written by someone who probably have never heard of? What is my credibility?

Let me tell you my story. My football education started at a very young age, I think I was four or five years old. My Dad was involved in a well-respected adult football team in Aberdeen called Mugiemoss. I used to go along with him and watch every training session and every game that they would play. I used to listen and watch everything that was going on, and this no doubt has had a massive influence in my thinking and footballing education. I remember being completely taken in by these players, they gave me attention and they were my hero's.

On days when there might be no games, my Dad would go scouting for new players. He was 100% committed to football and wanted to give it his best. Listening to him discussing player attributes was fascinating and has definitely influenced me to spot and develop talent and potential, and then help young players grow and develop.

"He has a good first touch, he is a good communicator, he is good in the air, strong in the tackle, he would fit in, he would give us something different"

Background and Introduction

The list goes on but the important message here and the first question of many to ask yourself:

How do you spot and develop talent and potential, what is your criteria?

One of the biggest influences that my Dad had in my football education was his intent and desire to "always give them (your players) the best, and they will give you their best back".

My father not only had a huge influence and impact for me but was widely and highly respected in the Aberdeen area. He touched the lives and influenced so many that after he passed away on New Year's Eve 2000, Dyce Juniors Football Club renamed their ground after him. (Mugiemoss had previously amalgamated with another club to form Dyce Juniors.)

The home of Dyce Juniors is now called Ian Mair Park, a fitting tribute and something that the family will be forever proud of. Amazing recognition of his influence.

What do you do to create the right and best environment for young footballers to grow and develop?

At the age of 10 I started to play football myself for the school on Saturday morning and then at the age of 13 I started to play Boys Club football. This meant that I was now playing football all day Saturday, and this was the next stage of football development, to listen to and learn from the many coaches I had in my playing career.

There were many different coaching approaches, but on reflection I think I learnt something from them all. Albeit in some cases, this is not the right way to do it!

I think in my playing career there were only two occasions that I chose to move clubs because I didn't enjoy the environment, I was in. It has to be fun (as well as development) and we all have a duty to create this type of environment that your children/players enjoy being part of.

There is a view that I am sure you can all relate to; you don't learn anything from any school teacher that you don't like. The same applies to a football coach.

Do all your players like and respect you?

I have many special memories of my time in youth football and I have many friends, lifelong friends and many special relationships created along the way through shared experiences and memories.

What memories and experiences are you creating for your young players… and for their parents?

From Youth Football, the natural transition is into adult football. This is a very different environment and it is important to develop players for this transition. Most of us will remember our experience and the change.

Background and Introduction

The approach to developing young footballers in the main has changed. You rarely see young children out playing football in the streets nowadays where they are really letting the game be their teacher. I didn't start youth football until U13, nowadays you can start from the tots age group. Grassroots coaches play an absolutely vital part as without organised football, how many children would play the beautiful game.

With the introduction of coaching badges and safeguarding children, the old school approach to the hairdryer route (Hairdryer routine of talking aggressively to players) is phasing out although still evident. Don't get me wrong, direct instruction and challenge still has a place. Our role is to get the balance right.

What would parents say about your approach to dealing with their children? Maybe more of interest, what reputation do you have amongst other coaches?

At a fairly young age, mid-twenties I suffered an injury that meant I had to stop playing. Tough to take, and although a few years and five operations later I did get back playing, football coaching and management was a necessary route for me to stay involved in the game and follow my passion.

I had the opportunity to do this with the team I was playing for at the time. It was a steep learning curve no doubt. Very quickly I had to adapt to getting my message across to players of different personalities and experience and I had to gain respect and credibility in doing so. Here is a life lesson that I have had…you gain respect by giving respect.

This is very different to starting out with a group of U5's, but equally challenging in delivering an effective instruction and or message.

I managed the adult team for 11 seasons, and I would like to think fairly successfully. The team progressed through the local leagues winning a few trophies on the way. It was competitive, it was about the winning…in saying that, winning in the right way by being a respected team and always wanting to playing football in the right way.

One of the most successful seasons was the one where I introduced a number of young 16 to 18-year-old players. I protected them and looked after them but trusted them as they were technically good enough. That season, we played some great football with a good blend of experience and youth. We won the League and Cup double!

At youth and grassroots level, are you all about the winning or the development of the players, or both?

After eleven memorable seasons I decided to stop because of different family priorities. I did always think though that I would go back to football management and coaching if I ever had a son or daughter who wanted to play football.

Background and Introduction

That opportunity did come along several years later. When my eldest son Lewis started school, he had an opportunity to join the local club's foundation and reception year team. He had already shown a real appetite and interest in football playing in the back garden.

On the midweek before his first session, I had travelled with a close friend Dave, to see to see Scotland play in Paris. James McFadden scored a wonder goal as Scotland won 1-0 away, a famous victory. The celebrations in the stadium with 20,000 Scottish fans were amazing.

On the Saturday I took Lewis to his first football session at the school. They had a game at the end and Lewis scored the winning goal. I can tell you that although I didn't jump about and celebrate… the emotion inside was the same as McFadden's goal. A very proud moment and a new football adventure was about to begin.

After watching the sessions for a few weeks, I volunteered to get involved, and not long after I found myself leading the sessions.

The numbers grew quickly and on some Saturday mornings there could be up to 30 kids enjoying the beautiful game. The club was called Milton Rangers. I had lived in Milton for a number of years and to be honest, it could have been any village that I lived in. I didn't really know anyone, but the involvement in football opened up a whole lot of new social interactions in the community. We have made family friends from this era.

We started to arrange a number of friendly games against other teams and at that young age it was really interesting to observe the children who were really up for football and those who, initially would prefer to make daisy chains and were there more just to be with their friends.

The next stage was to join the Mini League as an U8 team. I hadn't understood that I couldn't take all players and could only sign 12! Surely, I wasn't going to have to end football careers at this stage! Luckily, there were enough players to make up teams at two age groups U7 and U8 and therefore we could accommodate the majority. In saying that, I do remember a couple of players dropping out because of the family not wanting to commit every Saturday to football. There are far more opportunities available nowadays for children to try different activities.

It was a steep learning curve learning to provide the right and best environment which included a lot more than putting a team on the park to play football. Like me you probably have to … find a pitch to play on, a place to train, source a kit, arrange the games, line the pitch, set up a tea stall… the list goes on.

The football side alone was frustrating when things didn't go so well, but incredibly rewarding when they did. As we go through the chapters of this book, I will share my experiences and learning in more detail.

My approach is all about developing an intelligent footballer. I love to win, and in adult football it is competitive, and more about the results and winning. Don't get me wrong when the boys and girls played well and won it was great. However, we did take a few big defeats, and it is important to take this as an opportunity to learn rather than be upset with the players.

As the children played and continued to progress and develop, I learned a key question to ask parents after a game. For all parents of the children playing, here it is...

Would you rather the team won 2-0 and your son or daughter had a poor game ... or would you rather the team lost 2-0 and your son or daughter had a great game?

As I continued leading the team through U8, U9 and the most of the U10 season, this question asked occasionally enabled me to get into good conversations and to set realistic expectations of progress.

During the U10 season my son Lewis was offered a place at two different Academies. It was an opportunity that we could not deny him, and we accepted a place with Cambridge United. A very proud moment.

For the next five seasons I had the opportunity to watch, observe and learn from Academy Coaches. Countless nights standing in the freezing cold, miles and miles of travel to games and training. It was an amazing experience for him (and me) to play at top Premiership Clubs and

"Too often I hear it... clear your lines, you can't play football there and you see your players kick the ball up the pitch thinking tjhey are doing their job...winning games is for the coaches ego. It should be about developing technically gifted footballers"

John Collins

Omonia Youth FC

Background and Introduction

to go on European Tours. He no doubt developed as a footballer and person, no-one can ever take away from him the memories and what he achieved.

You can probably guess what is coming next. The same as what happens to 99% of Academy players, he got released. There was no awareness it was coming, particularly as you read the progress reports throughout the season. The way it was handled was harsh and brutal, by email with no dialogue and no face to face. There was no need for it to be that way.

As a coach and developer of young children and footballers we have a duty to treat them with respect at all times. Players will ultimately come and go at your club, but we should always be able to say hello and goodbye with equal amounts of enthusiasm.

As Lewis had gone to the Academy, I felt I had to resign from the role of Lead Coach at Milton Colts. The time commitment to meet the demands of Academy life would mean that I wouldn't be able to commit as much as was needed and in addition, I wanted to be there to support Lewis all the way in his football career.

However, ... six months later I found that I was really missing not being on the touchline on match days and in all the preparation for training sessions. I missed coaching and developing young footballers.

My youngest son, Daniel was about to start reception and foundation year at school. Daniel although less technical than Lewis at the same age, was keen to give it a go, and after a few sessions he was in the team and I volunteered to be the Assistant Coach. This meant that I could balance attention and development for both my boys. Being an Assistant Coach is different from being the Lead but can be equally rewarding in many ways.

The first ever game this team played together, they lost 20-1. I thought then that we had a big job on our hands but isn't that a great opportunity to challenge yourself and develop young children?

Fast forward to this season just passed, their U12 season and they have just won the League and Cup double. Their first full year in competitive Colts football. The development seasons and the time spent in the Mini League have seen rewards. Time spent coaching and developing the key principles of the game, the rotation, no set positions, equal game time and appropriate challenge. It was hard to stick to it at times, but you have to trust the process for the long-term benefits.

Do you rotate your players or have fixed positions? Do you give equal game time (before competitive football)?

Another great addition to the Milton Colts Part II was the introduction of a 'Tours' programme. I had wanted to do this with Milton Colts I and Lewis's team but ran out of time before he went to the Academy.

Background and Introduction

With Milton Colts II we have been to Aberdeen twice and Barcelona. In addition, one of the teams that we played in Aberdeen have seen the value and impact of being on tour and have since been down to Cambridge twice in return.

The development from going on a tour is significant. Learning about different cultures, style of play and coaching has had a big impact on both the players and coaches.

The memories created are priceless not only for the players and coaches but for the parents as well. It is downtime for them to have a mini holiday, but seeing their children have fun and develop not only as young footballers, but as young people is special.

Last season was very special for me in another way. I was given the opportunity to be the Lead Coach with Cambridge City U16's.

In the Eastern Junior Alliance (EJA) Lewis was playing with Cambridge City following his release from Cambridge United Academy. He had a good season in U15 where they had won their league section. More importantly Lewis was back to full fitness and was enjoying playing his football again.

The best way to describe the EJA is that it has players who have had Academy or Shadow/Elite Academy experience or who are high performing at Colts level. It certainly was a step up in challenge.

My job was to keep the team together, and to continue to develop the players. The objective given from the club was clear, "we would rather you finished 4th in the League and we had 10 players capable of making the next step to U18 rather than winning the League and we only have two."

A great challenge and clear objective and it is always good to have a clear objective.

What are your objectives for the season ahead?

It was a very special season for Lewis and me to share. It was probably our most enjoyable football season together. Lewis was Captain of the team that won the County Cup and finished runners-up in their League Section. Some of the football played was a privilege and a pleasure watch and to be part of.

At the end of the season all 17 squad players were given the opportunity to commence pre-season training with U18. My objective had been achieved as well as creating special memories and experiences. I am sure the Cup Final in particular will be talked about for years to come by both players and parents. I certainly won't forget it in a hurry.

Last season I also volunteered to run a Year 6 Schools Football Team. In the previous year they did not have a school team to play games and participate in tournaments.

Background and Introduction

One of the best, if not my best memory of primary school was playing schoolboy football with my mates. I wanted to create that same opportunity and memory for Daniel and his friends.

So, after doing all the necessary paperwork, I set up training sessions, arranged friendlies with other schools with teams with appropriate levels of challenge. It was great to see the children playing and having fun with their school friends in an environment that was not intense or pressured, I just let them play.

We did end up having a competitive team to play in tournaments. The boys who played came together from six different youth teams. I gave little instruction, just bought them together and let them play. They did actually win the South Cambridgeshire Tournament and reached the final of two other tournaments where unfortunately they lost both on penalty shoot outs.

At the end of term, we bought them all together for one last game at the school. Sometimes it is not all about the coaching, it is about creating the space and time for children to play and to let the game be the teacher.

At their end of year assembly before they headed off to the big school, the children did a mini play of their experience as a school team. I was proud that they did that, and I took it that for them, this had been a special school time memory and experience.

How much instruction do you give in training and games, do you have the balance right with instruction and letting the game be the teacher?

Nearly there...

I have also been the Vice Chairman at Milton Colts for the last three seasons and in that time led the creation of a strategy, vision and ethos for the club that was all about developing the intelligent footballer. This provided guiding principles for the coaching and development of players throughout the club and at all age groups.

Coaching and developing people is part of my professional work life. I am in a privileged position to be able to combine coaching in both sport and in business. There is a clear alignment in the design of business training programmes and football training sessions both with clear objectives to achieve. Coaching and asking the right questions for people to find the solutions for themselves. Facilitating groups working well together. There are many synergies in business and sport.

The final chapter in my incredible journey and experience. In 2020 I invested in a Franchise and became a Head Coach in the Milton and Bottisham community with the Football Fun Factory (FFF).

I have had a career in the corporate world of facilitating and creating the right and best environment for people to learn, grow and develop whether it be in the classroom, the Board room or on the Production Lines.

At the beginning of the year, I had the opportunity to review my career options and in a chance conversation with a colleague, they said "your face just lights up when you talk about football." This was an option that I had to explore.

I met with the founders of the FFF and I was totally drawn in by their compelling vision and strategy to be the world's leading football coaching organisation for young children. I had to play my part.

I now have the absolute privilege and pleasure to work with young children, to facilitate and create the environment for young children to fall in love with the beautiful game with some incredible memories and experience that will help them grow and develop...living the dream of being a full-time football coach!

Oh, last but certainly not least, the time spent on the terraces and football stadiums watching my club Aberdeen and my country, Scotland. I have so many special memories and experiences following club and country with lifelong friends and mentors. The endless football conversations, debates and days out were and will always be a big part of the education ... Thank you, Arthur, Simmy, Dave C, Craig, Rich, Lindsay, Derek, Dave T, Ray M, Ray C, Mark, Jim, Skeno, Ian and The Boom.

If you are still reading at this stage, thank you for staying with it. I am hoping by now that you will see that

I have a wide range of knowledge and experience to share with you. That at a minimum you have found the questions thought provoking and that you have already challenged or validated your thinking … and that you will have learnt something about yourself.

Enjoy the rest of the book as I go into a bit more detail and give you a deeper insight into my experiences.

In summary my football CV:

- ✓ My Father's influence
- ✓ Playing schoolboy and youth football
- ✓ Playing adult football
- ✓ Managing an adult team
- ✓ Lead and Assistant Coach, Milton Colts U6 – U14
- ✓ Observing Academy football
- ✓ Lead Coach Cambridge City U16
- ✓ Lead Coach of a Year 6 school team
- ✓ Milton Colts Vice Chairman
- ✓ Lead and Assistant Coach Cambridge City U13
- ✓ Learning and People Development professional
- ✓ Aberdeen and Scotland fan!
- ✓ Director and Head Coach Football Fun Factory community

What is your football CV?

Chapter 1: Why do you do it?

Why are you a football coach, why do you do what you do?

There are many reasons why anyone would want to be a football coach and I believe it is important for you to understand your reasons and motives as to why you do.

A number of years ago, I clearly remember after a training session with some of our U8 boys being challenged in our approach by a couple of parents. I believe it is important to be transparent and honest with parents and at some points also be vulnerable. We don't always have the answers and it is ok to say so, after all we are volunteers.

At this session I did feel challenged, if not a little bit angry as after all, like you all we give up a lot of time and we are volunteers. It did however push me to understand why I coach and develop young footballers.

Here are my reasons why I do what I do…

1. I want to give something back to the community and the beautiful game. Football has been very kind to me, and it is the game I love. Don't get me wrong it can be brutal, cruel and emotional, but overall, I have

had so many great experiences with so many special memories and have great friendships created through the beautiful game. It feels only right and proper that I give something back to the game and create new and special memories with and for others.

As mentioned before, living in Milton I could have been living in any village really, I didn't particularly know anyone. Getting involved in football opens up so many opportunities for social interaction and being involved in the community. It is a good and worthwhile feeling when you bump into players and parents in the local park or in the local supermarket in the village and they want to engage and talk to you. The feeling of being involved, a sense of belonging and that you are giving something back in helping others enjoy the beautiful game is a big driver for me being a football coach and doing what I do.

2. I really enjoy coaching and facilitating and seeing people grow and develop.

I think most of us would be able to relate the enjoyment we have had out of playing the game. Some will say that nothing can replace that buzz and enjoyment. However, I believe that if you get it right, coaching and helping people grow and develop does push it very close.

Of course, there will be many times where you feel frustrated, hard done by, underappreciated ... but learn

Chapter 1: Why do you do it?

to live with it and ride it because there are so many rewards to be had.

The buzz of setting up a training session with a purpose in mind, creating the right and best environment, asking the right questions for them to understand the beautiful game and for them to come up with the solutions themselves. This creates a positive and impactful learning experience. Think about it, this is a privilege.

Ultimately when the team goes on the park and they play with the tempo and touch, the desire and enthusiasm, the style of play that you have coached, and you have seen them improving, growing and developing confidence to do so, then that puts a smile on my face, and gives me a real sense of satisfaction and pride.

3. I want to spend quality time with my sons to create our own special memories.

For the majority of us, we are involved in running a football team because our son or daughter wants to play. Someone has to volunteer, and I would imagine that most reading this book will have a son or daughter in the team they are involved with.

I know this not the case for all but possibly is for most. Rarely at grassroots do you see a team being coached without a mum or dad of a player being involved.

Points one and two are very important to me but not as important as three.

As I know now time passes very quickly for the U5/6 to U16 and then they face the challenge of stepping into what essentially is adult football.

We want this to be a special memory of this period of their life that we will never get back. So much of who they are, and what they are will be as a result of your influence in this period.

If you are a mum or dad coach, it is tough at times. Your child will want your attention as they are used to at home when you feel obliged to give it to others. You will have to help them accept that you will give them attention, but it has to be equal in the team environment. It is all good learning about being part of a team. I have seen parent coaches be extra hard on their own child to compensate the fact they are the coach. Others have shown too much favouritism. I applaud you if you have the balance right.

You will also have a challenge depending on the level and how good your son or daughter is in the team. You are no different to any other parent, you want to see your child play and enjoy playing football. Getting the balance of appropriate and fair game for your child in the team is not easy and how that is perceived will also depend on how good they are.

Your child will be in the car with you to and from the games and to training. They will have to be there earlier than everyone else and normally leave last. It can be tough for them as well to be accepted. At Cambridge City U16 level, all three coaches had sons involved in the team. I spoke to the boys at the beginning of the season and said to them for me to pick them every week they had to be exceptional every week and in every training session both in terms of performance and behaviour. Thankfully they all rose to the challenge and made selection easier and without question from other players and parents. Credit to all three of them, they led by example and in fact, I believe contributed to the raising of standards of all the players.

You will have to challenge them and not show any favouritism. You must be even more honest with them in order to develop them.

I have learned many lessons along the way in people management and one of them is to always understand your why, why do you do what you do?

In summary of this chapter, this is why I do it.

1. **I want to give something back to the community and the beautiful game that has been so good to me.**

2. **I really enjoy coaching and seeing people grow, develop and be better as both an intelligent young footballer, and as a person.**

3. I want to spend quality time with my sons to create our own special memories and experiences…it has to be fun.

I think the 2018/2019 season was the best ever (to date) for both my sons in terms of enjoyment, development and creating special lifelong memories with them.

Why do you volunteer your time to run a football team? What are your motives and drivers, why do you do it?

I feel that it is important for you to understand and recognise your why, as this will help you shape your own sense of purpose and meaning.

It is a question that doesn't get asked that often and is one of the first steps in you becoming the best you can be.

Chapter 2: Being a Real and Good Coach

Being a real and good coach, what does that mean?

In the corporate world I have had the experience of designing and delivering a development approach called 'Our People Development Philosophy'. It does what it says what it says on the tin, it is a philosophy and an approach on how to develop people.

When delivering the programme content one of the opening questions to the participants is, 'how many of you have coached people in the workplace?'. Bearing in mind that all the participants are people managers and leaders, the normal response is almost always everyone.

When I then ask them, 'how many of you have used the GROW model?', the numbers drop dramatically.

The GROW model is probably the most popular and by far the best coaching model used in business... In my opinion.

The basic premise is, that if you are a true leader, asking the right questions will inspire people, to find their own solutions for themselves. Great questions should follow the outline of the GROW model and along the lines of:

Goal, what is your goal, what are you trying to achieve?

Reality, what is the reality of the situation now?

Options, what options do you have?

Way forward, what are you going to do now?

Now I am not for one minute suggesting that when coaching young footballers, you use the GROW model all the time, but I am strongly recommending...

That if we ask more questions, we can inspire our young footballers find the solutions themselves.

Take this as an example...

How many of you have seen the scenario where the goalkeeper passes or rolls the ball out to one of their team mates, they haven't checked their shoulder, they have been caught in possession, and then the opposition have scored?

How many of you have then, or seen the opposition Coach shout out instructions as to what they should have done, or worse berated them?

By asking them questions and then getting them to understand what else they could have done, it then becomes a learning experience that they will understand and possibly correct the next time.

Chapter 2: Being a Real and Good Coach

"I could open my body, take it on my back foot, check my shoulder, take my best option to keep the ball in the team".

Giving clear and directive instruction is not wrong, in fact it has a very valid place in the development of young footballers.

However, what we have to do is get better at asking more questions for them to learn and understand better from experiences and find their solutions themselves and learn about the game.

Do you have the right balance of asking questions, real coaching and giving instructions?
What ratio do you have between questions and instruction?

On another theme, I do believe that to get the best and most out of young developing footballers from a coaching perspective, you do have to set some clear guidelines and expectations.

If players understand the guidelines and expectations and this all happens as the norm, then you can invest more of your time to provide appropriate challenge to develop and improve.

We all know that with any group of young footballers there will be a wide range of behaviours and commitment, but if you can set your stall out with minimum expectations, then you have a great starting point to investing more time to continually improve and develop your players.

Do you have a minimum set of guidelines and expectations?

Here are mine as a benchmark:

Excellent timekeeping, I expect all players to turn up on time and be ready to train or play.

My brother-in-law has a good quote:

> **"You have no excuse for being late, you have had all night to get ready"**

Now we know that there are a multitude of reasons or excuses that people can use in today's world. In many cases it may not be the players fault but the parents! However, it is important to instil this discipline for the young children after all the same applies for being on time at school, college and in later life in the workplace. Effective time management or time attention is a life skill and discipline.

I also think that it is very important from an early age that the players take the responsibility for packing and getting ready their own kit. It is them who are playing the game and getting the kit ready, it is not the parents' job. Let them learn and give them the responsibility. If they forget their boots and can't play, I am sure they will learn and not make the same mistake again. I have seen it happen on numerous occasions believe it or not!

Chapter 2: Being a Real and Good Coach

The welcome handshake. I expect all my players on arrival to immediately come and shake my hand. It gains and builds respect and lets me know that they have arrived, and that they are ready to participate. It also lets me know if all is not right for example, an injury or illness.

Next, I always check for correct kit and in particular for clean boots. It is a pet hate of mine… dirty boots. It is about taking pride in your appearance, representing your team and your club. I have a quote:

"Look good, feel good, play good"

It makes sense, doesn't it? I love to see young children taking pride in their appearance and I believe that it helps them feel good and it plays a part in amplifying their odds of playing well. Taking it further and into adult life, this is another life skill and discipline on personal hygiene and dressing for success.

It is important to give players downtime and space to enjoy each other's company and have some social interaction.

However, it is important that you draw the line between that and your time to coach. I call it 'my time' to talk. I recently heard a player say quiet to his teammates, "it's Mike's time". I liked that and felt it is part of developing respect and trust both ways. Give them the space and permission to enjoy being young children but at the same time ensure that you help them understand the value of respect and when it is time and allow only one person to talk at a time.

When it is my time, the instruction and questions are clear and don't take too long. It is important to be clear and articulate and to keep the players attention and engagement.

Some of the techniques that I have used include:

- The rule of three, no more than three key messages
- Use of coloured 'posts it's', to make the point
- Use of a tactics board, making it visual, and as they say a picture paints a thousand words
- Sticky messages, repeating the same message so that the players remember it and eventually apply it

Finally... maximum effort is a minimum requirement. I expect players to want to learn and be there, to enjoy the challenge to improve and be better and therefore it is not unreasonable to expect maximum effort. If players see improvement and they feel it, then so will the parents. If the culture and values align with maximum effort being the norm, then real development starts to happen.

So, as a benchmark, how do you compare, and do you have others of your own?

- **Excellent timekeeping**
- **Taking responsibility for their own kit**

Chapter 2: Being a Real and Good Coach

- **The welcome handshake**
- **Look good, feel good, play good and in particular always having clean boots**
- **My time to talk**
- **Maximum effort is a minimum requirement**

The players, the developing young footballers are now ready to be coached.

In coaching there are a few other approaches that I use to get the best and most out of my players.

Set appropriate challenges to develop and improve.

What can we learn from our last game, what went well, what could we do better?

This is a fundamental question that I always ask myself after a game and then often to the players the next time we get together at training.

Learning from mistakes and experiences fast tracks development in my opinion.

If we can collectively talk about" what did we do well?", and "how can we be better?". It opens up the dialogue to develop intelligent footballers. I also find this is a positive way to develop ourselves as coaches. We don't always see what the players see in the game.

Nine times out of ten, after pre-season, when we concentrate on working out and setting the style of play and formations, the next training sessions should be about creating dialogue on the last game and preparing for the next.

Repetition of learning and key messages does have a big part to play in embedding key skills and attributes. As coaches we can deliver the same message but in different ways and in different situations and scenarios.

It is important therefore that you develop drills and sessions that continue to engage and challenge our developing young footballers but at the same time it does no harm, only good to repeat sessions to embed the learning.

Be heard (and be understood)

Being heard doesn't always mean at the top of your voice. Yes, at times we must be loud to get players attention. We may also have to get instruction from one side of the pitch to the other in a timely manner. However, if you have to have the balance right, just as powerful is the quiet time, softly spoken in the changing room before a game or when you get the youngsters to calm down and settle down.

The key point is to use and choose the tone of your voice, so that your message is understood.

Recently I observed a Colts League Manager berate loudly his young players at the end of a game. "you didn't listen, why didn't you do what I asked?"

Chapter 2: Being a Real and Good Coach

> *"I've learned that people will forget what you said, people will forget what you did, but people will never forget how you made them feel"*
>
> **Maya Angelou**
> **Poet**

Go on, be honest, we have all either done this or seen it?

To be honest I didn't understand the point he was trying to make and so there was little chance that these youngsters would have. It was a cold day and they had just lost a game.

Take time to reflect on the quote on the previous page and how it resonates with you in developing the intelligent young footballer.

Next time you deliver a message, take time to reflect… was I heard and was I understood… and how did I make them feel?

I have three other things for you to consider in your approach to coaching and getting the best and most out of your players.

Number one, always be alert to spot and recognise application of the learning of your players. Last week in a game, the wide right player bust a gut to track back and help his full back. I know this was in the pre-match instruction, but when he did it and I recognised the contribution, he did it in numerous other occasions throughout the game and I expect he has now learned the value of this application and contribution.

He recognised it and felt the importance. Hopefully I made him feel good about his contribution, but

Chapter 2: Being a Real and Good Coach

probably more important, he had learned the value of this aspect of the game for his teammates and his own development.

Here is a challenge for you in your next game. Spot and recognise three particular contributions. Let the player know you have seen it, let the team know you have seen it and then watch the reaction and the responses.

How did it make them feel?
How did it make you feel?

Number two, always be there to listen, be available and approachable.

There is a lot going on in the lives of young people nowadays. I do feel at times that they must be overwhelmed with information overload. Be it at school/college, social media or sport... we need to give them the space to reflect and assimilate information.

It is important that we give them space in group conversations. Ask them questions and ask them to reflect on recent results and performances. A good practice that I adopt certainly as the children get older is to ask them to feedback on the last game played. This is a good practice as it gives them time to reflect and to hear the thoughts of their teammates and their coaches.

You can be sure that most parents will have already had a conversation about the game with their child whether it is in the car on the way home or over the dinner table.

For this reason, you are giving them the opportunity to share their own thoughts and that of their parents and you then get the chance to challenge or validate their thinking.

In addition, always be available and approachable for the individual and one to one conversation. This is an important component in building relationships and trust. Let your players know that they can come and talk to you and to ask you questions.

What ratio of your coaching time with your players do you spend in a group situation versus one to one?

Finally, surprise them!

Consistency and standardisation, familiarity, routine and comfort are all very important aspects in developing the intelligent young footballer.

The element of surprise, challenges them in different ways and ultimately develops them. We all know that taking people slightly out of their comfort zone, in the majority of occasions develops them.

Change your pre-match routine approach, change your team talk, give them a gift, get them some new kit. Fairly simple things to do but you could be even more radical.

Last season with my U16 team I surprised them with a jazzercize class, on another occasion I invited a guest coach and on another when the team thought they were turning up for a training session I actually had a friendly fixture organised.

How innovative and creative can you be to surprise your players?

So, in my summary from this chapter in being a real and good coach:

1. **Ask them questions to inspire them and find their own solutions**

2. **Set appropriate challenge to develop**

3. **Be heard and understood**

4. **Be approachable and be there to listen**

5. **Set expectations**

6. **Recognise contributions**

7. **Surprise them**

8. **Make them feel good**

> *"Coming together is the beginning, keeping together is progress, working together is success"*
>
> **Henry Ford**
> **Industrialist**

Chapter 3: Have a Transparent Recruitment Policy

How do you recruit players to be part of your team or club?

I suppose a lot depends on what stage you are at. Personally, and based on experience, I think that there are three distinct recruitment periods.

The first is when first setting up and starting a new team and I am talking about at Under 6 (U6) or U7 or even U5 at some clubs. For me this is about being all inclusive, all abilities and giving all aspiring young footballers an opportunity. At these age groups we really don't know where these young children are going to end up, at what level they play and in fact even what positions. It really is all about creating an environment where their first experiences and memories of football are special…after all, nobody has excelled in the game without first falling in love with it.

When my eldest son Lewis first started off at Milton Colts I could see that there was real energy and enthusiasm in the group. They were fun and prepared to engage and learn. Sometimes you are lucky in getting a good group early on.

When my youngest, Daniel started there was also a lot of energy in the group, and they couldn't wait to get started with games... In their first ever game they lost 20-1! I can remember talking to Darren, the Manager and saying we have a real job on our hands here! But isn't that great, isn't that what it is all about and a real challenge for you in developing intelligent young footballers?

In this game that they lost 20-1, Daniel was really happy that he nearly scored. I still haven't had the heart to tell him to this day that he was going the wrong way and just as well that he missed, otherwise it would have been an own goal!

At the time they were an U6 team. With a lot of patience and support, the core of that team has stayed together and developed into a team that won a League and Cup double at U12 and nearly repeated it at U13 by winning the League but denied the chance to repeat the double by the national lockdown during the Covid-19 Pandemic of 2020. They had made it through to the Cup Final that unfortunately for them was never played. It would have been another great memory and experience for them but we all accepted the importance of Safety and the impact of a Global pandemic certainly put everything into perspective.

Yes, some players left, football wasn't for them and others joined along the way, but the core stayed. The time, patience and opportunity to work with them to develop not only as a team but as individual players was very special

Chapter 3: Have a Transparent Recruitment Policy

and shows what can be achieved in terms of developing the intelligent footballer.

We never actively recruited any players taking the view that we develop what we have got. This approach can be incredibly rewarding.

If you are involved from the ages of U6 to U12, do you actively recruit, or do you take the approach to develop what you have?

Based on experience, I think the second distinct period is around the U12 to U14 mark. This is when most teams transition to competitive football, when cups are there to be won and lost and League points matter. It is also the period when teams make the transition to 11-a-side and inevitably need more players.

I have experienced a real mindset shift of players, coaches and parents. Football is always competitive even at the younger age groups. It always will be as long as there are two goalposts on the pitch. Players want to score and score more than the other team. Younger than U12, I think in the main you can work on the development and get away without the results really mattering.

However, from U12 on, everyone knows the results, and everyone gets to know the levels of appropriate challenge. Good players want to play with and against good players. All players want to be at a level that has appropriate challenge and I think that development is hampered if you are continually playing in the 10-0 games, whatever team you are in, the team scoring 10 or conceding 10.

As a coach do you want your team to be winning well every week, or would you rather you lost every now and again?

We all know that a lot would prefer to be winning every week, but for me being tested and being challenged creates the environment for everyone to grow, develop and be better.

As I said, at U12 to U14 there is normally a need to recruit as most teams start to make the transition to 11 a side and to do that successfully you will need a bigger squad.

This is a challenging period as most teams will have formed and built relationships. New players create a different dynamic and how to manage to integrate them is important.

It doesn't matter what team it is, in business and sport they all go through the stages of team development.

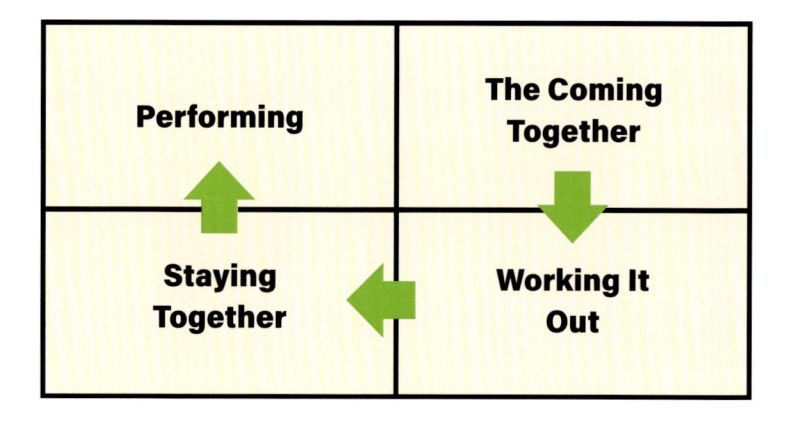

Performing	The Coming Together
Staying Together	Working It Out

Chapter 3: Have a Transparent Recruitment Policy

The coming together, the beginning.

The *working it out* is when everyone works out their place and role, who they like and don't like (initially) and what I prefer to call meaningful conflict and all part of team development.

Staying together is when players, coaches and parents come to terms with the norms, embracing the challenges and opportunities and new ways of working together and a way forward.

Performing, when it all starts to click into place, everyone gets to know the strength and attributes and the team begins to perform and enjoy being together.

What stage of the team development model is your team?

There are no given timelines as to how long all this takes to move from the coming together to Performing. The important thing is to recognise what stage you are at and what you need to do to accelerate the development.

There is another stage that is often referred to. The stage being 'Mourning', where a player leaves the team. This is a natural thing to happen for any number of reasons. This could include family relocating, wanting to join a 'better' team, wanting to go and play with new friends or wanting to pursue a different activity for example, athletics, rugby or dance.

Whatever the reason, it can have an impact on young children, which is not to be underestimated. We have to support them through the change and for many this could be their first experience of change.

We are all enthusiastic and energetic when recruiting players, but when they choose to leave you should consider this… I like to think that as coaches we should be able to welcome players and say goodbye with equal amounts of enthusiasm. When a player leaves, I feel that it is our duty to leave on good terms. This is all part of our role in creating special football memories and experiences…you never know, they may end up coming back at some stage!

Our goal as coaches is surely to enable young footballers to play at the highest level they can, for as long as they can that they enjoy.

It has to be fun for both, the players and the parents. I don't believe that any parent wants their child to be in an environment that they don't enjoy and are not happy.

Sure, there will be tough times and tough days if performances and results don't go the way we would want.

In a recent game we played, our boys although they played really well in stages of the game, were all disappointed at the end of the game, as they lost.

There was some great application of learning and development from the previous game. I was naturally disappointed with the result but really pleased with the performance. For the boys the result was a surprise and did not meet their expectations.

Chapter 3: Have a Transparent Recruitment Policy

At the end of the game in the changing room I opened the floor to them to ask questions and or tell me how they felt. Very interesting perspectives from the eyes of U13 developing young footballers.

When was the last, time you gave the whole team, together, the opportunity to ask you questions and tell you how they feel?

And if you did, did you listen to understand, or defend your decisions and choices?

The third and last distinct period of recruitment I think is at U16 leading into U18.

It is interesting watching children growing throughout the age groups and all at different rates. We all know at younger ages some games are won and lost purely on physical strength and not by technique.

However, by the time they are U16, most are starting to grow into their adult bodies. This means that for physically strong players there is a levelling out. This is where the investment in technique starts to pay off because technically good players with physical attributes flourish.

At U16/U18 many players find other interests and commitment. Some look for jobs, others focus on education. You will also find that some start to prefer socialising and parties and therefore cannot be as committed.

I also think at this age groups there is a decision to be made by the players as to how serious they are about the beautiful game.

Some will want to play for fun and with their mates.

Others will want to be more serious with one eye on progressing to adult football.

There are conflicts at this stage though. At an U16 game recently the Manager of the opposing side asked if he could keep his players behind in the changing room after the game for a few words!

I said that I didn't think his team had been that bad... however he said that he was going to explain to them that they can't play schoolboy football, Colts League football and more senior football. The growing body can't cope with the demands and the players have to choose what level they want to play at...

Young footballers/children should be able to play at the highest level they can, for as long as they can, that they enjoy.

It is great to be involved with a less serious team where boys and girls enjoy are playing with their friends, in a team but don't take it too seriously. If you are creating that environment, then good on you and I applaud you. As well as creating special life long memories and experiences at the early stages, it is as important and the end of grassroots children's football experience before the next transition to adult football.

Chapter 3: Have a Transparent Recruitment Policy

What is your most memorable season/ time in football as a player?

I wouldn't mind betting that for many of you it was in Youth football…now it is your time to return the memory and give something back.

Always be honest and transparent and as players find their way, their level, inevitably you will be recruiting at these age groups.

To summarise, I think there are three distinct periods for recruitment, in the beautiful game, U6, U12 to U14 and U16/18.

Our role at each of these periods is to attract players, retain them for as long as you can and develop them.

I started this chapter by asking if you had a Recruitment Policy. Although not written in tablets of stone, this is my policy I use as a guiding principle…

- All local based players in your community should be given priority option. However, this may still be based on ability and potential if you have large numbers, but you must try to do everything you can to include and give the opportunity.
- At all age groups do not exceed maximum squad size that you can sign on. In doing this, you give yourself a better chance of giving the right amount of attention and keeping all happy with the amount of game time (both the children and parents).

This may appear harsh but the more you sign, the more you have to keep continually happy. In this instance rules are rules and use it to your advantage. If you can sign 14, sign 14 not 16.

- Players should be signed with appropriate challenge in mind. The players need to be able to participate and develop at the level the team are playing at and that they would not dilute the quality of the squad.

Good players want to play with good players and trust me at whatever age, they can work it out. You have a duty to develop at appropriate levels.

- That they fit into the culture of the team and that they can build good relationships.
- This applies not only to the players, but the parents.

If you are to be trusted to develop the young footballer, it is important that you can engage and build dialogue with the parents. It is their child; they want the best for them. Engaging with them and building relationships helps.

Most of you will have come across the term 'the pushy parent.'

I know of some coaches who purposely want to keep their distance and not get too involved with the parents.

This is my approach, I prefer to build relationships.

Do you build relationships with the parents, or do you keep your distance?

Chapter 3: Have a Transparent Recruitment Policy

"The triumph can't be had without the struggle"

Wilma Rudolph
American Sprinter

Have you ever not signed a player because the of the parent?

In summary my Recruitment Policy as a benchmark is:

- **Give priority to local children (particularly at the early age groups)**
- **Do not exceed maximum squad size**
- **Sign for the appropriate level of challenge**
- **Do they fit into the team culture?**
- **Do the parents fit into the club culture?**

As I said, not written in tablets of stone, just a guiding principle.

How does your Recruitment Policy compare?

Chapter 4: Let the Game be the Teacher

OK, we all have to give instructions, set up drills and guide our players to the best of our abilities. All of this is a given and part of being a football coach.

However, I am a great believer that we have also to let the game be the teacher.

Most people who know me would say that I am fairly disciplined and that I have high expectations of the players that I am involved with.

Does the same apply to you, are you disciplined and have high expectations and if so, what are they?

To be honest, I expect the answer from most of you would be yes, in your own way.

Ok, so let's accept that for the most of us we have set disciplines and expectations of our players.

With this in mind, let me challenge you, and ask how can you create the environment and the balance to let the game be the teacher?

When talking to friends from my childhood era, we agreed that there actually was very little coaching in that period and we probably learned most playing football in the streets and parks. There were a lot of good players from that era. We had fun and made great lifelong friendships based on the shared experiences and memories that we created together.

Unfortunately, you don't see many children playing football in the streets nowadays and occasionally in the parks. As coaches I feel we should still create the space and time to let the game be the teacher. Let them experiment and learn from each other…and give yourself a break to just enjoy watching them.

Here are my guiding principles.

Set up the drills to let them experiment, try new skills and increase the tempo. If players can feel it, they will believe it for themselves. You have to get the balance right of intervening to give instruction and just letting it go and happen.

Most of my football learning and education happened playing in the streets and parks with friends. We used to pick teams, play games like 10 half time, 20 the winner and then we would swap sides and start all over again. There was not a coach in sight, the game was being the teacher.

It is very different nowadays of course. We don't see children playing football in the streets and parks. Many young children wouldn't even go near the game if we

Chapter 4: Let the Game be the Teacher

didn't do what we did in setting up organised football. Well done for setting up your organised group and thank you for doing so and facilitating children learning and having football experiences and memories.

Don't lead all the time, challenge yourself to let the session go and let the game be the teacher.

You have to enable the young footballer to find 'the IN', the first thing they need to do to help them learn the new skill.

My favourite story and best example is young children learning to do keepy ups. This is can appear a daunting task and can be disillusioning for many particularly if they see others doing it well. I can remember feeling inadequate because I couldn't do as many as others and then spending hours on my own practicing and trying to get it right.

Now helping children get started, by giving them the first 'IN', I get them to hold the ball in their hand, drop it onto their foot and bounce it back up. This 'IN' comes from a learning technique called Micromastery.

Micromastery focusses on finding the 'IN' and then letting them experiment through 'PURPOSEFUL PRACTICE' which then leads of a 'PAY OFF', new learning and a competitive advantage for them, for example the keepy up.

It could be a great new tool and technique to help you in your approach to coaching, it certainly was for me. If you can learn and understand the concept, it has so many potential applications in the game. Micromastery is a unique way of accelerating the learning into doing.

Let the player's experiment. One keepy up will then become two, three and confidence will grow and build. You have given them their first IN and the will to feel the development themselves.

Let them learn from their mistakes and don't always intervene. Really difficult I know, and I have done this myself on many occasions and not felt good about it afterwards. I think I have learnt a lot about my approach and really do not accept berating players. If it does happen and let's be honest on occasions it will happen in the heat of the moment, I always apologise and help the players understand perspectives. It may not be immediately, more often than not with me it would be at the next session, but these occasions thankfully are now few and far between. I have learned that you have always to be thoughtful with your words and actions.

Accept and appreciate that this will happen, but it should never be the norm.

You must help the players learn from their experimentation and their mistakes otherwise they will not learn and develop. Do it in a way that helps the learning and not through fear and reprisal.

As coaches most of us are probably prone to giving a lot of instruction but let them work it out for themselves.

If we are to develop the intelligent footballer, at times we need to let them work it out themselves. To be honest,

Chapter 4: Let the Game be the Teacher

this is probably more relevant as the players get older, certainly for U14 onwards.

In a U16 game last season our team was under a bit of pressure. One of the coaching team was enthusiastically giving instruction. I asked him to stop. If we trust the instruction, we gave them in the dressing room, we should trust them to learn and develop and at times this means let them work it out themselves. We passed on a few words, reminded them of the task in hand and they sorted it. As another one of the coaching team said, "this is great development for them", and it was.

We talked it through post-match and I could tell that they were very pleased with themselves, both individually and collectively.

Have you developed your players by just leaving them to work it out themselves, if so what happened?

Don't over complicate it. When giving instruction I really try to never give too much information. As a personal discipline I always try to keep it to the 'rule of three'. It is a proven technique that if you give instruction in threes, there is a far better chance on the message and instruction to be understood.

Challenge yourself, try it out and see what happens. In your next game or training session, try and deliver the message using the rule of three.

For example, what are the three things that we want to achieve in the game today?

In a game last weekend, the three key messages for this particular game were to…

- Defend (and earn the right)
- Shape (keep the shape and discipline)
- Create (make chances to score)

The team talk was relatively short, but the three key messages were made clear. I set the expectations and gave the opportunity to ask questions to clarify roles and responsibilities.

Post-match and the debrief, did we defend, keep shape and create goal scoring opportunities?

The young developing footballers demonstrated intelligence through discussion of the application and recognition of what and how they had achieved what the game plan was. Very rewarding and real for them and great positive learning and development.

If you were a fly on the wall, would you think that your team talks were over complicated or, about right?

Don't talk too much, it is not about you. Giving too much information complicates things and of course it also

Chapter 4: Let the Game be the Teacher

has an impact with concentration levels depending on the age and maturity of the players.

You are 'presenting' a message, you must keep your group engaged and you must give them an opportunity to assimilate the information, take it on board and then apply it.

Next time you give information either at training or on match day observe two things.

First, how long did you talk for and was it appropriate to the age group and maturity of the players? In my experience start, stop is better with the younger age group. Longer is ok with the older age groups as their concentration levels will be higher hopefully and they will be trying to assimilate and take on board the information.

An interesting observation for me is that certainly when they get to U16, the better and more confident players will start to debate and challenge you back. I think this is great, embrace it. It will help you develop your communication style and it will help them understand the beautiful game more as you reply and get deeper into explaining reasons why.

Second, observe the body language of the players. Are they paying attention, are they engaged, are they listening and understanding?

In communicating with young footballers, you have a 'simple' task, to be understood.

If your message is understood, then you are playing a big part in the learning and development of the player.

Be very much aware of your words, your tone and your body language and the body language of your players.

I believe that activities in training and in pre-match warm ups must be game related. By all means use fun and enjoyable activities to help you create a fun learning environment. These activities can be used as energisers and then serve a purpose. The purpose being:

- To build team relationships, and a sense of belonging
- Providing a safe environment to explore and experiment

Back to the game related activities to enable and allow the game to be the teacher.

Play and practice like you aim to play in the game to develop the touch and technique and do it with pace and tempo. Practice and training should be fun, but you should train and practice like you aim to play.

Do it quick… but never in a hurry. Think about it, there is a difference.

Being able to play at pace and tempo in the long term gives your players a competitive advantage. If they can do it in training, then you are amplifying the odds that they will do it on match day.

I sometimes give my players a challenge, to pick a partner in training and then at the end of the session give them time to have a discussion as to who trained the best, listened, tried new things and worked for the team. Peer to peer feedback and conversation is

Chapter 4: Let the Game be the Teacher

a positive aspect of developing the intelligent young footballer.

Sometimes they will listen and learn more from each other than the coach! They always want to be competitive with each other and it develops good practices.

Repeating sessions and messages I feel always adds value. Repeated messages become 'sticky' messages that if heard often enough will help embed the learning.

What are your 'sticky' messages to your players, what are the things you always say to them?

I always find it pleasing and rewarding when you hear players repeating the message, it means that they have listened, understood, taken it in and that they believe it, they see and feel the value and the purpose.

Repeating sessions enables players to see and feel personal progress. I don't mean repeating every other week but repeating often enough that players remember and can relate to the purpose of the session.

In training, if players, your players are progressively developing and getting better together then the tempo and technique will increase. Players normally see and feel progress, and even more so if they can see and feel the application in game time. It becomes real for them.

As well as being good football coaches we also have to be good people managers. It is important to recognise, acknowledge and reward progress, but always be mindful that some players are not getting it as quickly as others. This may mean giving additional support at a session. I would also consider giving 'homework' for development.

For example, I had one player whose first touch on the backfoot was not as tight as others. I asked him to go home and practice as often as he could and wanted to. I asked him to play the ball off a wall as he could be sure that the wall would pass the ball back to him. He could listen to music of his choice to make it fun if he wanted. Clearly, he practised and within weeks there was a marked improvement and he felt great about it, you could tell by the smile on his face when he was getting it right and I took every opportunity to let him know that I recognised and observed his application and learning.

Just one point for you to consider in this chapter.

I always feel for defensive players in training and practice. We are big on skills and always encourage it in training. As important is the skill of defending and tackling.

We calm this down in sessions so that we can avoid injury yet come match day, we expect our players to be skilled and good in the tackle. We encourage our players to be skilful and to experiment with as many as they can in training. However, we normally ask our players to calm down with the tackling in training!

Chapter 4: Let the Game be the Teacher

How do you develop the balance, for attacking and defensive players?

Practicing defending also becomes a challenge depending on the surface that you train on.

In training and of course on match day, I encourage players to stay on their feet and only slide tackle as a last resort. This in turn develops their reading of the game and their positional play.

For defensive players, the ultimate is to protect their goal and if we can get them to delay the play for others to recover, defer the play away from the goal and then to intercept then that should negate the need for too much tackling in training. In saying that, as players get older, defending and winning the ball effectively becomes very much part of the game.

To let the game be the teacher, here are my guiding principles:

- **Let them experiment and enjoy the game**
- **Don't intervene too often let the game go and flow**
- **Let them learn from each other**
- **Let them work it out themselves, challenge their thinking**

- **Don't overcomplicate instruction and make use of 'sticky messages'**
- **Open up the dialogue, talk about and discuss football**
- **Make all activities game related**
- **Repeat sessions and messages to embed and let them see and feel the progressive learning**
- **Set appropriate challenges for development**

One last thing to add in this chapter, I think that it is important that the players and children recognise and appreciate the part their parents play.

I always encourage at the end of the games, win, lose or draw that they go over together and applaud the parents. It is good learning for the children and I know that it is appreciated by the parents.

Chapter 5: Be Interested in their Development

Have you ever heard the term 'Diamonds and Vehicles,' being used in football?

If you haven't here is my understanding.

The '**Diamonds**', are the star players, the ones who have perceived real potential and are likely to get a lot of attention. The Academy coaches like them because they could be the next best product of their system. The grassroots coaches like them because they are the ones most likely to win the game for the team.

The '**Vehicles**', are all the other players needed to make up the numbers so that you can put a team on the park to play. The Diamonds can't play on their own and so every team will need players to make up the numbers. At Academy level, they will still be very good players and more than capable of playing at the level, they just won't be the ones who will be perceived to make it at the highest level. At grassroots, every team needs a squad of players and many will be signed to ensure that you have the numbers and squad to cover when players are injured or perhaps on holiday.

Now I not saying that every team is formatted in this way but challenge yourself.

Do you have 'Diamonds' and 'Vehicles', in your team?

The real challenge for coaches like you and I is that we have to be interested in the development of all our players. The development of the Diamond us equally important as the development of the Vehicle and can be equally as rewarding.

Let's stop using the terms, Diamond and Vehicle, personally I don't like it, but it is reality. Real development for me takes the following format.

```
     ┌─────────────┐  ┌─────────────┐
     │    The      │  │  Building   │
     │ Individual  │  │    and      │
     │   Player    │  │ Developing  │
     │             │  │  The Team   │
     └─────────────┘  └─────────────┘
            ┌─────────────┐
            │    The      │
            │ Environment │
            │ to Learn and│
            │   Develop   │
            └─────────────┘
```

The Environment to Learn and Develop

By this I am meaning the best it can be with the facilities and resources available and accessible to you. Included in this is your personal growth and development and being

Chapter 5: Be Interested in their Development

better and evolving the environment that you create. Here are some of the things that you should consider in creating the right and best environment.

You should always have at least one ball per player and a good set of cones and bibs. Not forgetting that you must always have a fully stocked First Aid Kit at every session and game. The environment should always be welcoming and engaging and always with safety in mind as a priority. If you create the right and best environment this will amplify the odds of the players giving you their best back because they want to be there and that they enjoy what you have created. I always get there early to set things up and, in many ways put on a show for the players and parents as they arrive. Having everything set up creates a good impression and gives you the time to relax and get in the zone yourself.

How welcoming and engaging is the environment that you create both for training and on match days?

I always shake the hand of each player as they arrive, and I always get eye contact with them. As adults we learn how to meet and greet people. Doing this at an early age is helping them learn this life skill. It also means that with this discipline you can give every player the attention and respect that they deserve.

(Note, the handshake was not possible during Covid, and different approaches to meet and greet were applied).

Preparation, "fail to prepare and prepare to fail", a good quote that I continually refer to.

If you are setting up for a match day, I always like to have the pitched lined before every game, corner flags out, goalposts in place long before anyone arrives. This normally means getting up early in the morning, but I feel it is all worth it both for your team and your opponents…and it allows you to relax and enjoy watching the children play football.

The Individual Player

It is important that you give each individual player in your team due care and attention and develop each and every one of them no matter what level they start at.

It is your job and responsibility to develop all players.

It is great if we develop a player to go onto bigger and better things and achieve a lot in football. Equally rewarding is the player who enjoys the game, plays with a smile on their face and incrementally gets better.

With the older age groups, thinking U13-U16 it is possible to have great development conversations with both player and parent. A lot depends on how serious you are. A reality check is that I think from U13 there starts to be a separation of the teams, those who are more serious and competitive and those who want to play more for the fun and the social aspects of the game.

Both are as important as each other. For some having a development conversation is just a bit too much. However,

Chapter 5: Be Interested in their Development

if you can, I have found real value in having meaningful development conversations.

I always involve the parent and a good conversation facilitates:

- Setting appropriate and realistic development challenges
- Setting appropriate and realistic expectations for the season
- Understanding what the player enjoys
- Understanding what the player would like to see improve

It provides a focus and can be a review of progress and provides clarity and is transparent. It also starts to prepare them for adult life as in the business world, performance and development reviews will become the norm. Involving both the player and parent and getting them to articulate and engage in conversation develops the understanding and appreciation of the game and the intelligent footballer.

Building and Developing The Team

It is important to create the environment for an engaged and happy team and where they enjoy being together. Children are children and inevitably there will be issues that you will need to deal with and handle appropriately. However, in general terms there are a number of things that you need to consider in getting the balance right:

- Provide a welcoming and engaging environment
- Be inclusive and treat all players with respect
- Have no favourites
- Develop all players
- Set collective team goals
- Be fair and consistent in your decisions
- Provide a fun learning environment

As a benchmark and comparison, how does this compare to what you do? Is there anything different that you do?

It is important to set expectations of what it means to be part of a team. I am all about developing individuals but equally important is developing a team ethic.

If someone joins your team, what are your minimum expectations of them in being part of a team?

Here are the expectations that I set:

- That they attend and participate in all training and games. We all know that for various different reasons people may miss training or games and if it happens occasionally, it must be accepted at grassroots level, but it shouldn't be the norm. If they commit to being part of a team then they need to be there to be part of it and that includes training and match days.

Chapter 5: Be Interested in their Development

- That they are on time and if appropriate with the correct kit, which includes drinks bottles and clean boots.
- That they enjoy themselves and have fun but equally that they are prepared to be challenged to develop and be better.

I feel that as teams come together and stay together it is important that you create the space just to enjoy each other's company.

Being part of a team can feel pressured for some and at times 'just' turning up to train and play doesn't give the social space to correct, engage and develop relationships.

What do you do to create the social space and downtime for your team?

Here are some of the approaches that I have adapted over the years.

- Mixing the players up in activities so that they are not always with their best friend. Here is a technique that I used. Go around the group and tell them that they are either:
  - Super
  - Fantastic
  - Brilliant, or
  - Great

  "Can all the 'Super's, get together, all the 'Fantastics', all the 'Brilliants' and all the 'Greats'. They all then start asking who is 'Great' etc. "I am a Great" and eventually they get together and then feel good about the fact that they are 'Great'. There is no conscious or unconscious bias in the selection and a great way of mixing the group and developing relationships.

- Asking them questions and ask for their feedback. It is a really good approach to opening up and valuing dialogue. Done well, it allows you to listen to understand and to further connect and engage yourself. It will give you opportunities to hear what is valued and potential areas to improve. Above all, if it becomes expected that you will ask, it really can fast-track team relationships and building trust. I start this at a young age. Sometimes you don't get a lot back, but stick with it, it's fun and pays off in the long run. Children can be very honest!

Remember the model that I shared earlier:

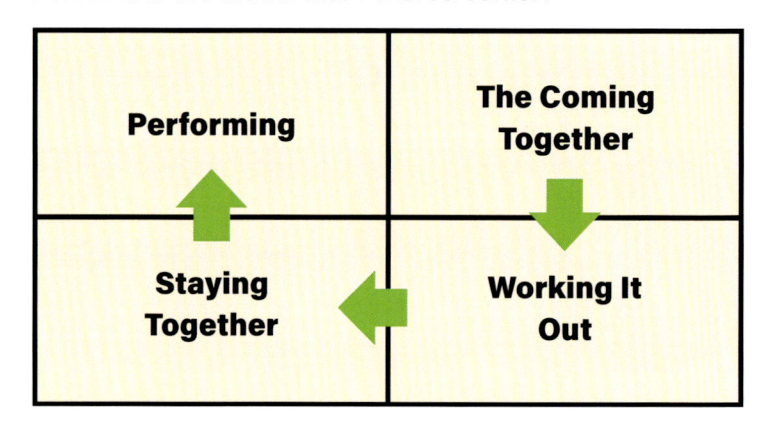

Performing ↑	The Coming Together ↓
Staying Together	← Working It Out

Chapter 5: Be Interested in their Development

> "I always tell my players to find the fire within themselves. A chance like this will never come around again. Seek that fire, don't be ashamed of it, if anything they demand to dream."
>
> **Claudio Ranieri**

Here are a few other things to consider helping get more from the coming together to working it out, building relationships and moving into the working it out and then the staying together stages.

- Invite players to come early or stay later so that they can practice on their own, let them do their own thing and let the game be their teacher, and give them the space just to be friends. Of course, in most cases this relies on the flexibility of the parent, and so be careful not to create an environment where any player can feel left out.
- When training, give them extended drinks breaks. Again, it allows them space and downtime, their time to talk and just be friends. It could be football related or it's more likely to be their latest exploits or FIFA or Fortnite! Recently at a session with young children they were all trying to rescue the worms on the astro turf! Can't remember covering any of that on any coaching training programme…it was funny. Extended time also gives you the time to set up the next session. Personally, I sometimes find it a bit pressured setting up between drills to ensure the session flows. However, if you create the time and space so that it feels part of the overall plan, I find it really does help. If you have the opportunity to give the players space and time in a changing room environment, use it. I have found that it adds a lot of value, to get them their good time before

Chapter 5: Be Interested in their Development

kick-off, usually 45 minutes to an hour before. This means that there can be a good warm up and team talk time, getting the team in the zone to play and enjoy. It also allows them time to play their own music, chat, sit next to who they want to and build relationships.

This is all part of developing the young footballer but there are a few things you must consider ensuring the environment is conducive to what you want to achieve.

- Safeguarding is always your priority and leaving young footballers really does depend on the maturity of the players. Based on a few experiences here is where it can go wrong…

    I once came back in and one of the players had accidentally smashed a light doing keepy ups. It clearly had upset the young lad and his team mates. Not best preparation for a game never mind the safety issues. A changing room will be full of characters vying for position and status, you just need to be clear on what is and not acceptable behaviour in representing themselves, their team and their club.

    Not every player likes music and so it is important to engage the team to create a 'team' playlist that will appeal to all and not switch some off.

    I have found that extending the time on their own gradually gives them the ownership and responsibility for their time and provides some very clear boundaries from their time to game preparation and my time to name the team and give the final instructions which always includes "enjoy the game."

I don't encourage the use of phones. I think they are distracting and affects the concentration levels of young players. They are there to play football not play on their phones. There is also a concern about safeguarding and photography in the changing room. I know that players will still have their phones with them, but my experience is that as the maturity of the young players grow, they self-police and it is not an issue.

Beyond the training sessions and match day it is recommended practice to create pure social time. This is both applicable to players and parents.

I know that some coaches are not keen on building relationships with parents, but I think this is really important in providing the best fun, learning and safe environment for their child and for you to create the best shared footballing experiences and memories.

Have you created some pure social time for your team and parents, if so what?...

Most teams and clubs will have the end of season, Player of the Year event. I am a great believer that:

> **"If you do not celebrate success, you will have none"**

Chapter 5: Be Interested in their Development

For that reason, it is important to create this space and time to recognise the progress and achievements individually and collectively.

Most young players enjoy voting for their Player of the Year and I think they in the main are genuinely pleased for their team mates who are recognised.

The range of trophies 'presented' can be wide but it is important to do it for both the players and parents. It is a social gathering that for some is the highlight of the year, particularly for community clubs.

Throughout the season I would suggest doing different activities with the purpose of social downtime and building relationships.

I remember a quote during my time in adult football:

**"Those who drink together,
win together"**

Now, not for one minute am I suggesting alcohol related activities but the learning for me clearly was that spending time together builds relationships in teams.

Golf, mini-golf, footgolf, swimming, sports days... these are examples of some of the things that I have done with good effect with different teams at different age groups.

Whatever you do it also has to be age appropriate. In the early years you will find that when young children have birthday parties, often they will invite the whole team or at least some. I tend to let that flow and only really from U12 on do I think I need to get involved in setting up social non-football related events.

One significant development that I have had experience of is the introduction of a Tours programme.

Although first appearing to be expensive it can become less so if the team engages in fundraising activities. The fundraising itself becomes fun and I have seen things like, team quizzes, sponsored park runs, car boot sales and bag packing at supermarkets.

Tours are great experiences, not only for the football but in experiencing different cultures and really feeling being part of something.

I have had the experience of going to Scotland, Holland and Spain. For both the children and parents a successful tour can add so much to life experiences, creating memories and developing the intelligent young footballer.

If you haven't already done so, have a look at both UK and European Tour and Tournament options. There are plenty out there and these become a great opportunity to create memories.

Finally, Summer Tournaments. There are many Summer Tournaments for teams to participate in. Personally, I like to get the balance right of choosing a few to keep the players together but also giving the time off from football.

Chapter 5: Be Interested in their Development

What is your approach to Summer tournaments, none, a good balance, many?

I used to think that young children can't get too much football and would be happy to play in numerous Tournaments.

However, I have changed my stance on this for a couple of reasons.

- The children/young footballers need recovery time and the time to do other things like giving other sports a go like athletics and cricket.
- The parents need a break from all the driving and travel.

So, it can be a complete Summer break, a good balance or effectively non-stop football.

It is important that you understand your players and your parents and to adjust your approach accordingly. There is no right or wrong, but my preference is, not to overdo a good thing and to get the balance right.

As much as I love football it is also something that I have learned, is that I need the downtime and a break just to keep me on top of my game.

How do you give yourself the space and downtime to recharge your batteries and keep yourself on top of your game?

To let the game be the teacher, here are my guiding principles:

- **Develop all players**
- **Develop the environment**
- **Develop the individual and have great development conversations**
- **Develop the team and set expectations of being part of a team**
- **Create some non-football related social space and time**
- **Continue to develop yourself**

Chapter 6: Have a Clear Strategy and Vision for your Team

What and where do you want to be and by when with your team and or your club?

In this chapter I will ask you a lot of questions to challenge and validate your thinking on your strategy for your team and or your club.

Some may think that this is not necessary, but I would challenge that. Even at a young age, it is about you setting out your approach or what you want to achieve in a clear and transparent way for both players and parents. It helps them understand and support and buy in to the vision where they can also see and feel progress as well.

Don't we all engage with, have a sense of purpose and meaning to what we are doing and engage with a sense of belonging, being part of something?

In the early years I am very strong in 'teaching' and giving the young footballers the environment to learn and develop new skills. My particular favourite is helping them learn how to receive the ball on the back foot. In the long term it will be of undoubted and competitive benefit.

I can recall a U8 game a number of years ago. We had just played a game and we had 'lost' to a strong and direct team. Throughout the game we kept playing the ball out from the goalkeeper encouraging all players to find space, get on the ball and to receive it on the back foot.

There was a 'scout' from a senior, professional club watching, and he said that it was very rare to see all players in a team at this age group and at this level being brave enough and for most being comfortable to receive the ball on the back foot.

The more direct team who for various reasons, I don't think that they are still together now, whereas we are and are recognised for always wanting to play football from the back and take the ball on the back foot. It is a clear and transparent strategy and vision that the players and parents have bought into from an early age.

We shared the conversation with the 'scout' with the parents after the match and asked them to trust us. Most young children can kick the ball and chase it and will kick it harder and run faster as the grow bigger and stronger but if they never learn the back foot and ball mastery, it will delay their progress and enjoyment of the game long term.

I am not saying that my model is right it is just what I believe in. The following questions will help you have clarity in your approach and once you have that, why not share it with your players and their parents. You will have a

Chapter 6: Have a Clear Strategy and Vision for your Team

strategy and vision and you will know what and where you want to be and by when with your team.

- Are you set out to be a competitive team with a win at all cost's mentality, or is it about fun and development over winning? (Certainly, in the early years and if so when does it change, at what age group?)
- Do you adapt your approach season by season or do you have a long-term strategy? For example, from U8 all the way through to U18.
- Are you recognised for being a direct and strong team or as a team who always want to play football?
- Are you prepared to accept defeats for the long-term development?

This season I expect that the new Cambridge City U13 will not be the strongest team in the League. There are some very good players, but they have only just formed as a team. They are having to learn and adapt to new team mates, bigger pitches, for some it is their first season at 11 v 11, more travel, playing against better players and teams. It can be a steep learning and development curve and I accept that, but with the view that all players have potential and that they will have developed by the time the team reaches U16…as long as they continue to enjoy it.

- Do you want to be measured by the trophies you win or by the style of football you play?

- Do you actively recruit to get the best players, or do you invest time to develop what you have? Development over results.
- What type of players do you like to develop, the big strong ones, or the ones who have technical potential or both?

When looking at potential, here are the sorts of attributes that I look for:

- Can they receive the ball in different situations and positions on the pitch?
- How good are they at taking on board information and learning?
- Have they got pace?
- How good is their ball retention, can they keep the ball in the team and pass it with purpose?
- Have they got a range of skills that they can apply in different situations across the pitch?
- Are they brave enough to both get on the ball and tackle?
- Are they coachable, do they want to grow and develop?

Being able to learn and apply these attributes does depend a lot on the opportunities that you give them to develop.

Next two questions:

1. Do you rotate your players, or do you have fixed positions?
2. Do you give equal game time, or do they have to earn the right to play?

Chapter 6: Have a Clear Strategy and Vision for your Team

These are all interesting dilemma for all coaches.

In theory, at a very early age when teams are playing 5-a-side, you should be rotating players in all positions in a diamond formation.

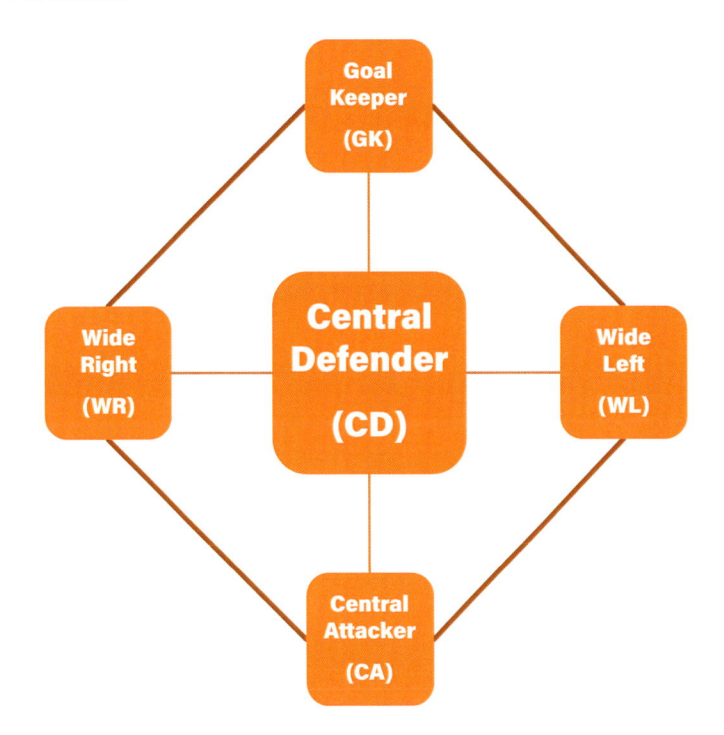

```
                 Goal Keeper
                    (GK)

    Wide Right    Central      Wide Left
      (WR)        Defender       (WL)
                    (CD)

                Central Attacker
                     (CA)
```

Being a goalkeeper (GK) is not for everyone. Some love it, others hate it, but every team needs a goalkeeper. Unless you have one child who really wants to be a goalkeeper you should rotate to give all players the appreciation and experience.

At a young age we don't really know the natural abilities of each player. How at the age of six or seven, can we say that a young child will end up being a striker or defender? If we give them the opportunity to rotate and learn, yes, they will eventually have a preference, but I believe it is our duty to give them the opportunity to experiment. If we do there are clear advantages long term.

- ✓ It helps the player learn and grow in confidence.
- ✓ It gives an appreciation of and understanding of the game from a different perspective.
- ✓ It enables you the opportunity to spot and develop their potential.
- ✓ It gives them the appreciation and understanding of what it means to play their part in their team.
- ✓ It gives you flexibility to rotate when players are not available.

Looking at the advantages, if you can develop players to receive the ball wide, right and on the left and in a central defending or central attacking positions you are developing the full player and preparing them for all eventualities.

In the modern game, that is played with pace and agility, it requires players to be comfortable on the ball in all situations on the pitch.

Don't get me wrong I am not saying that fixed positions from an early age is wrong. It is just not my preference. Having fixed positions gives a different opportunity to

Chapter 6: Have a Clear Strategy and Vision for your Team

continually learn all aspects of a position and to potentially excel at it.

However, in the long term as the players progress from 5-a-side to 7s, to 9s, to 11s, they will have to learn the new and different positions. It is only at 11 aside that they are really starting to prepare to play to their strengths. Even then, challenge yourself.

Can the player be equally comfortable and competent in at least two positions on the pitch?

There are many stories of players playing in a fixed position but then changing and becoming successful in another position. For example, in my opinion the greatest player that I have seen play... Willie Miller.

Now I know that I am being completely biased in my opinion but as a young player and in his teenage years, Willie Miller was an out and out striker. He had signed a professional contract for Aberdeen as a striker but at some point, he changed and converted to become a central defender.

He captained and led Aberdeen to Scottish and European success in the Alex Ferguson era. Aberdeen was the most successful team in Scotland in that era and won two European trophies beating Bayern Munich and Real Madrid on the way. I know, almost unthinkable that could have happened, but it is true. Aberdeen was recognised as being the best team in Europe and Willie Miller was widely recognised as being the best penalty box defender in Europe.

The point is we should rotate players because at a young age we can't really predict where they will play when they are an adult.

Although I am a strong believer in rotating players at an early age, it can be fraught with difficulties.

My view is that you should continue to rotate players until about the U15, U16 season and then develop them in their strongest/preferred two best positions.

Let me outline some of the difficulties in taking the approach to rotating players:

> Some children start to prefer positions and don't want to play in a position they don't like even though the intent is for their development.
>
> For example, the right sided player playing on the left to develop their touch with their left foot.
>
> In a recent U16 season I had two very good wide players who played on their preferred right and left sides. I introduced them to the concept of swopping sides occasionally throughout the game and being the inverted wide player. At first there was a bit of resistance, understandably having played there a lot in 11 v 11 seasons. They both bought into the development opportunity and could see the benefit of cutting inside on their 'stronger' foot. It developed a whole new skill set and their reward was that they both scored more

Chapter 6: Have a Clear Strategy and Vision for your Team

goals than in their previous seasons. They both went onto have the ability to play on both wide positions both as attacking players, but also learning their defending and tracking back responsibilities.

- Parents start to prefer positions that they see their child playing in. A lot love to see their child score the goals or not having the perceived pressure of having to defend. Equally though I have seen parents love the opportunity to see their child play in a different position. For example, the child who has always been the defender, watching them have the opportunity to play further forward. I had a young lad recently who although only 12, had been taught to defend and play right back and would barely cross the half way line. Once the shackles were released, his Dad loved to see him getting forward and joining the play and enjoying doing so.
- Coaches start to see strengths in players and without being aware, change their strategy to pick the stronger players in their best positions to win games.

This will naturally happen over time but at what age have you shifted your strategy of rotation to fixed positions?

It is of interest that in recruiting for a new U13 team, I am really keen just to let the players play in the open sessions and have a look at their player potential and intelligence, but I am already being fed information on their positions with them just coming out of the U12 season.

This is of interest because as we work with players from a very early age, we get to know them, but to have them in set positions at 12?

How do you manage the game time of your players?

Do you give them equal game time allowing all to develop, or do you always play your strongest team?

When I was running Milton Colts U8, in our first season of being given a set of League fixtures, I had the big learning and 'aha', moment of what I should do.

We were playing an away game and I made the mistake of getting caught up in wanting to win the game. No matter what the result was going to end up being, there were no official league placings, no points, but most coaches know the results and keep their unofficial leagues... don't they?

It was a tight game; it was very cold and wet and there was one player I only gave the token gesture of playing the minimum number of minutes in the game. He was a good lad but at that time probably not my strongest player.

At the end of the game the Father came to me and asked why his son had not played more than the minimum minutes. The look on his face was one of

Chapter 6: Have a Clear Strategy and Vision for your Team

disappointment and it had a profound impact on me. I gave some poor excuse and reason, but in the car on the way home I felt bad and I made a decision to ensure that all players would get at least half a game going forward.

At the training session the following week I spoke to all the parents and applauded the one who had come to me. I explained my reflections and learning and my 'new' strategy going forward.

I feel that I had demonstrated being transparent and to a degree vulnerability and opening the dialogue was appreciated and accepted. It built trust and buy in no doubt. We stuck with it in all League games and friendlies all the way through to when I left near the end of the U10 season...but there was a twist.

In that same U10 season there was a competitive cup introduced. We were doing well in it progressing to the quarter finals.

On the day we were 2-1 up at half time in a tight game. I had started with a strong team as we were all learning to 'compete' in a cup. However, at half time I made the three substitutions that I had committed to do in League games and to keep with the strategy of at least half a game and fair game time.

I remember the two other coaches giving me a look and asking if, I was sure. One of the children to come on was the son of one of the coaches, the other one was the daughter of the other. I was sure, I had made the commitment. How do players develop if they don't get game time?

We lost 3-2 with the last kick of the ball to the eventual cup winners. One of the coaches despite it being his own son said at the end, "you didn't need to do that, it was a competitive game".

Many years later we still talk about that moment. Had we denied the opportunity for those young children and parents to experience being competitive and winning? Could they have gone all the way and won the cup?

The point of these two stories… as a coach it is really difficult to get the balance right. My new reflections and continued learning:

- Players won't develop if you don't give them game time.
- As you progress through the age groups, you need players to be comfortable playing. If at 5-a-side you only give your 5 strongest most game time, at 7-a-side you will be challenged as 5 good players won't 'win' a 7-a-side game.
- Being involved in cups is competitive. Give yourself permission to develop in all league games but challenge yourself and them to learn and develop in what will ultimately become a competitive game and a competitive world.
- Always be open and transparent with players and parents. You need to work with them… and if they don't like or buy into your strategy… They have a choice.

Chapter 6: Have a Clear Strategy and Vision for your Team

- Knowing when to change or adapt your approach. It is great to have a strategy and intent, but you also have to be able to adapt and adjust and not to have a fixed mindset. The game is constantly changing as is the needs and expectations of people, the children and the parents.

What would you like your team to be known as and recognised for?

Here are some of the terms that we probably have all used at some point to describe opposition teams:

- They are a physical team
- They are very direct
- They play the high press
- They play out from the back
- They keep possession

What others can you think of?

We also all can be more specific about players if we know them from playing them in the past…

- They have wide players with pace
- They have a great goalkeeper
- They have a strong defence
- They have a good striker

This is all part of the game and I like to think that the majority of the time in children's football it is out of respect and no malice. I do enjoy getting in to conversations with coaches of other teams about their players and giving recognition where it is merited and noticed.

What reputation does your team have, how would you describe your team and their style of play... how would others describe your team?

If you have coached a number of teams you will also gain the reputation of the style you play.

I always want to play out from the back. More players get touches on the ball and more players are developing and learning.

Last season when coaching a new team, we were playing against a team where I had known their coach from a previous team. Less than two minutes into the game I heard him calling to his players, "remember they will always look to play it out from the back and so press high".

I didn't know how I felt about that initially. Great credit and recognition that my teams will always want to play football from the back... but have I become predictable?

My strategy and approach will always be to play football and we will just have to learn and develop to play against teams who give the high press. Of course, part of player development is to understand how to change and not be so predictable?

Chapter 6: Have a Clear Strategy and Vision for your Team

The last part in this chapter is to consider your approach and strategy to playing different formations through the age groups. Every coach will have their own preference.

What are your preferred formations playing through the age groups, from 5-a-side, to 7, to 9 and eventually 11-a-side?

At 5-a-side for me it is definitely the diamond:

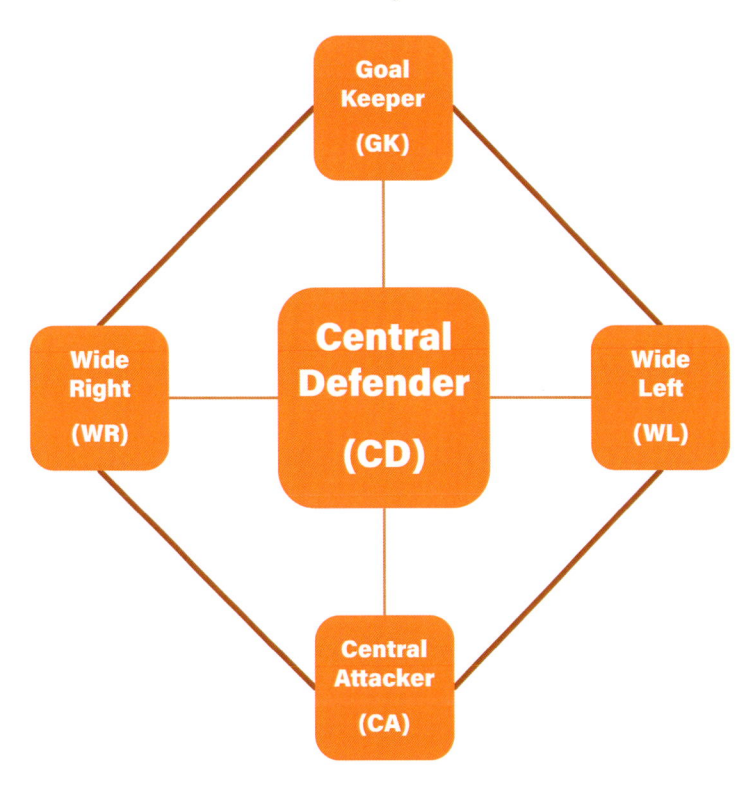

```
            Goal
           Keeper
            (GK)

Wide                    Central                   Wide
Right                   Defender                  Left
(WR)                                              (WL)
                         (CD)

           Central
           Attacker
            (CA)
```

As previously mentioned, rotation gives the opportunity for all players to play all positions and from an early age, learning to understand the space and to receive and distribute the ball.

As we progress to 7-a-side my preference was then to play 2-3-1.

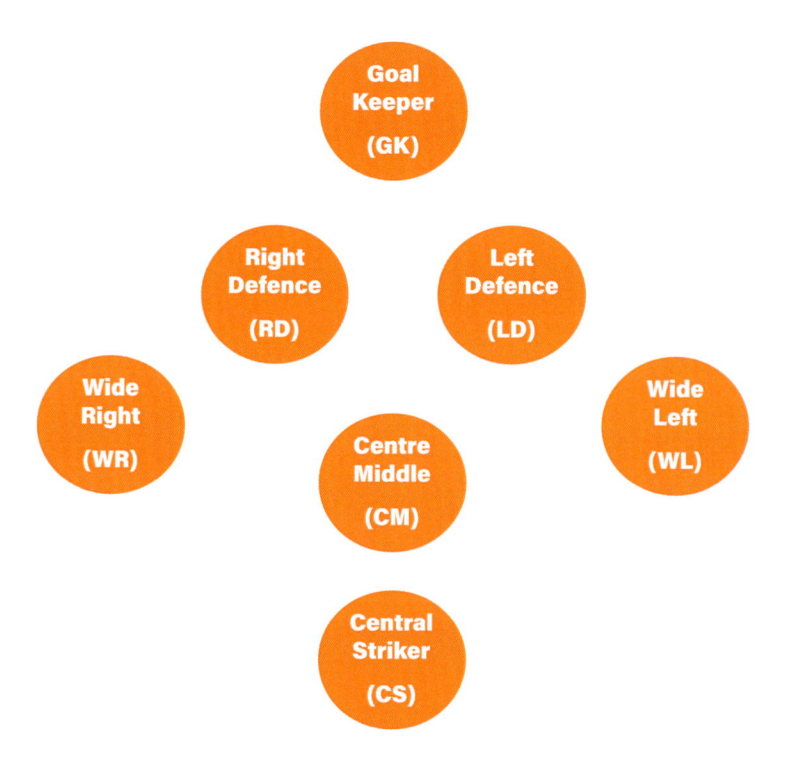

```
                Goal
              Keeper
               (GK)

        Right         Left
       Defence      Defence
        (RD)          (LD)

 Wide                         Wide
 Right         Centre         Left
 (WR)         Middle          (WL)
               (CM)

              Central
              Striker
               (CS)
```

The reason for this was to continue the development through playing the Diamonds. Assuming your central

Chapter 6: Have a Clear Strategy and Vision for your Team

striker would drift slightly to the side of the park that the play was… you would then have a diamond shape on that side of the park, e.g.

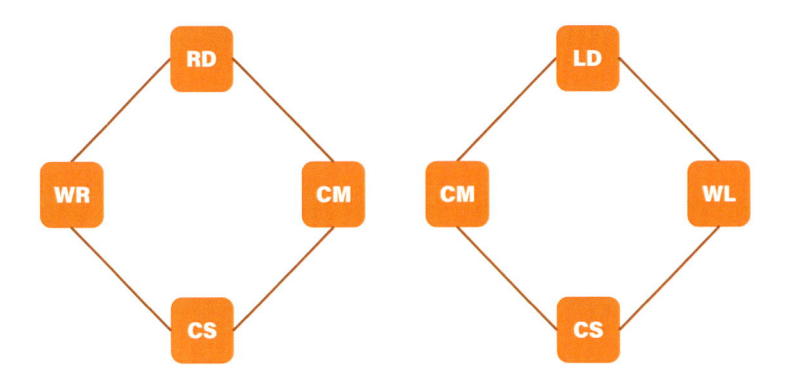

```
        RD                         LD

WR            CM          CM            WL

        CS                         CS
```

It is a continuation and development of the message from 5-a-side and continues to develop players as right and left sided players and central both in midfield and as striker.

There are many variations at 7-a-side that you could play, and you will have your own preference, but I feel that the 2-3-1 is the best for player development.

As well as the continuation of the diamond formation it also continues to develop the spatial awareness across the pitch. In particular for the wide players and their appreciation for the need not only to play forward but be aware of their responsibilities to track back and defend.

The next progression is to 9-a-side. Again, there are a number of different formations to play but my preference at this stage of their development is the 4-3-1.

At first glance, this may be perceived as a defensive formation, but the intent is far from that.

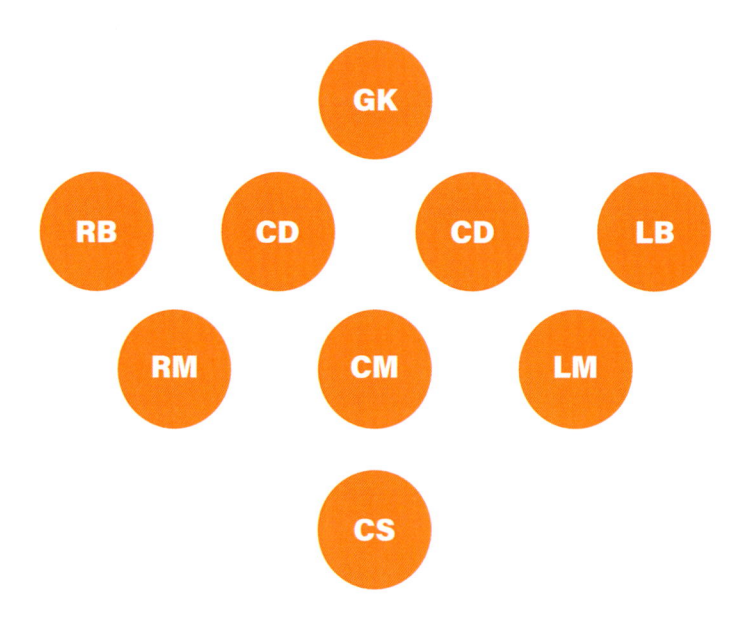

For the RB and LB, this really is the opportunity to be both the wide defending and wide attacking player and aligns with the role and responsibilities of the modern full back.

At 9-a-side this is where you start to develop the principles of operating in a back 4 and the responsibilities

Chapter 6: Have a Clear Strategy and Vision for your Team

to working and communicating together, covering each other, following the play and the slide across the field, the distances between each other and of course defending.

The same principles apply to the midfield players and also includes who goes forward, and who sits and covers.

I really enjoy the 9 v 9 phase of their football development. You start to see the benefits and application of all the development prior and you start to see the development, understanding and intelligence from the young footballers. It is also a great preparation phase for the next stage of transition to come, 11 v 11.

This formation in my opinion is a continuation of the learning and encourages playing football and still getting as many touches on the ball as possible. As the pitches get bigger, with the players utilising more space the long ball may be played. Don't get me wrong, there is always a place for the long pass, but if we are still focused on the development, then we still have to touch the ball as many times as possible. Personally, I would like to play 9 v 9 at least until U15 as these players have the rest of their life to play 11 v 11, they won't get the short lived 9 v 9 time again.

Playing with a back 4 is a first step in preparation for 11-a-side. I know that there are variations to play with a back 3 or a back 5 but I feel the most used formation is starting with a back 4.

Playing with the back 4 encourages the GK to play out from the back and then for the rest of the team to engage and connect to play football.

There are plenty of reference books out there if you want to learn more about tactical formations. I am not going into any great detail about the formations I prefer, I am just suggesting what is best for the continued development of a football, possession-based team in my experience.

At 9-a-side, this is also the age to really develop the thinking with regard to the transition with and without the football. It also starts to challenge their thinking that the work without the ball is equally as important as the work with it.

For young footballers, my preference is that they stay on the smallest pitch they can for as long as they can. It encourages more touches on the ball and as I said they will have the rest of their lives to play 11-a-side.

In the Cambridgeshire FA, we had the option to go 11 v 11 at U13. A lot of teams took that option, but we stayed at 9 v 9. I think that was best for their personal and team development.

At each stage of transition, the bigger pitch is always a challenge, more space and more running. They will inevitably develop their spatial awareness and their physical fitness. Don't miss the opportunity to continue to develop their technique and touch.

Chapter 6: Have a Clear Strategy and Vision for your Team

Now to 11-a-side, what is the best formation for their continued football development?

Before I share my preferences, it is important to point out two things.

- It is good to have a preferred formation to play, your strategy, your vision, but for pure player development you should change your formation for some games and in stages of games occasionally to give the full development experience. In Youth football, 'your' player will leave you at some point. Let's say they are now progressing into adult football and the team they join plays a 3-5-2. If they are a defender and they have never played in a back 3, then they will be at a disadvantage for their understanding and appreciation of the game. Have a preferred formation but mix it up every now and again for player development and appreciation.
- It may depend on the players that you have available to you. There is no point in being stubborn with your strategy and preferred formation if you don't have the players to fit the formation. For example, if you have a squad of let's say more defensive minded players and few strikers, playing 4-3-3 with three strikers may not be your best option… unless of course you want to develop that skill set.

My preferred 11 v 11 is 4-2-3-1:

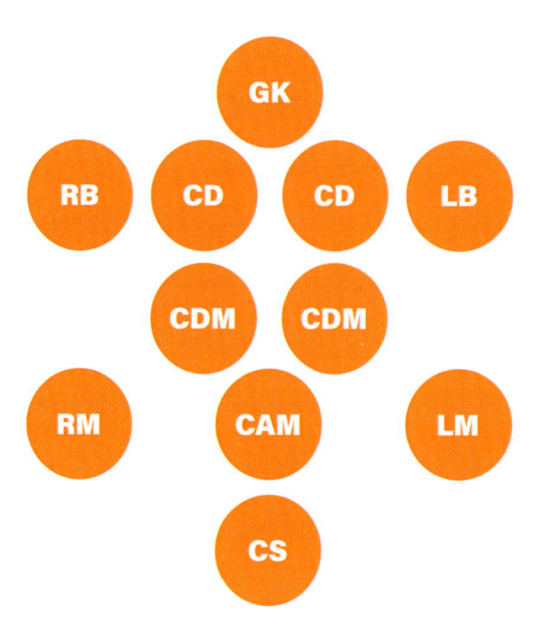

```
            GK
    RB   CD   CD   LB
         CDM  CDM
    RM       CAM      LM
             CS
```

The reason for this is based on what I said previously about players being close to each other and playing possession football.

It gives a real balance of defensive strength and creativity going forward. It is very agile for the transition, with or without the ball. Players can drop into shape and position to defend and very quickly transition to be an attacking force. It hopefully builds on and continues the message and development of playing football.

I like to develop teams to dominate the game both in and out of possession, 4-2-3-1 is very fluid and supports both.

Chapter 6: Have a Clear Strategy and Vision for your Team

With Cambridge City in the U16 season, they were playing in an important league game. We lost possession and very quickly, the team understood their roles and responsibilities and dropped into shape. The options for the opposition to play were vastly reduced. We let them have the ball and the shape of the team was a joy to see. We regained possession and very quickly became an exciting attacking threat. This was near the end of their U16 season and it was an absolute joy to watch and observe. Great development, understanding and appreciation from them as intelligent young footballers. Each player knew the part they have to play with great awareness and work ethic.

By the time they get to U16, 4-2-3-1 is my preference... but I feel it can be too complicated for the first season at 11 v 11. Don't over complicate things.

For that reason, I think at U13 when most are making the transition to 11 v 11, It may be best to start with 4-4-2. The young footballers have the challenge and the steep learning curve of playing on the bigger pitch and with bigger goals. For many for this reason it may be a bit overwhelming to start with and easier to make the transition.

I feel 4-4-2 is the continuation of the development and eventually you can start to challenge them with different formations as their fitness, strength and appreciation grows.

Some would say start as you mean to go on and go for the more complex formations early. It is all about appropriate challenge and if you feel that your players are ready, by all means go for it. It would certainly accelerate the learning and the development.

In summary, I think it is important that you have a strategy, vision and style of play that you share with your players and parents. Having a plan in your mind about formations is part of the vision.

Do also bear in mind that changing it up every now and again is also great learning and development and you want to provide your young footballers with an appreciation of playing football in a variety of positions and formations.

Remember the challenge I set earlier, by the time you get to U16, each player should be comfortable and competent to play in at least 2 different positions and in different formations.

You will have prepared them for the next step into U18 and adult football wherever it takes them.

A tool and technique that I have found useful in developing the intelligence and thinking of a young footballer is the decision tree. I will share an example with you and you can take this and apply it to any situation in a game.

The example is about having possession.

It can be easily drawn up on a wipe board or piece of paper. It is best practice to set up the challenge and then get the players to talk and populate the boxes together. It both accelerates and embeds the learning and they own it.

This is a real example, used with a U12 team. You can of course prepopulate the content if you want to lead and make

Chapter 6: Have a Clear Strategy and Vision for your Team

a specific point. Whatever way you want to use it, it certainly encourages interaction, participation and ownership.

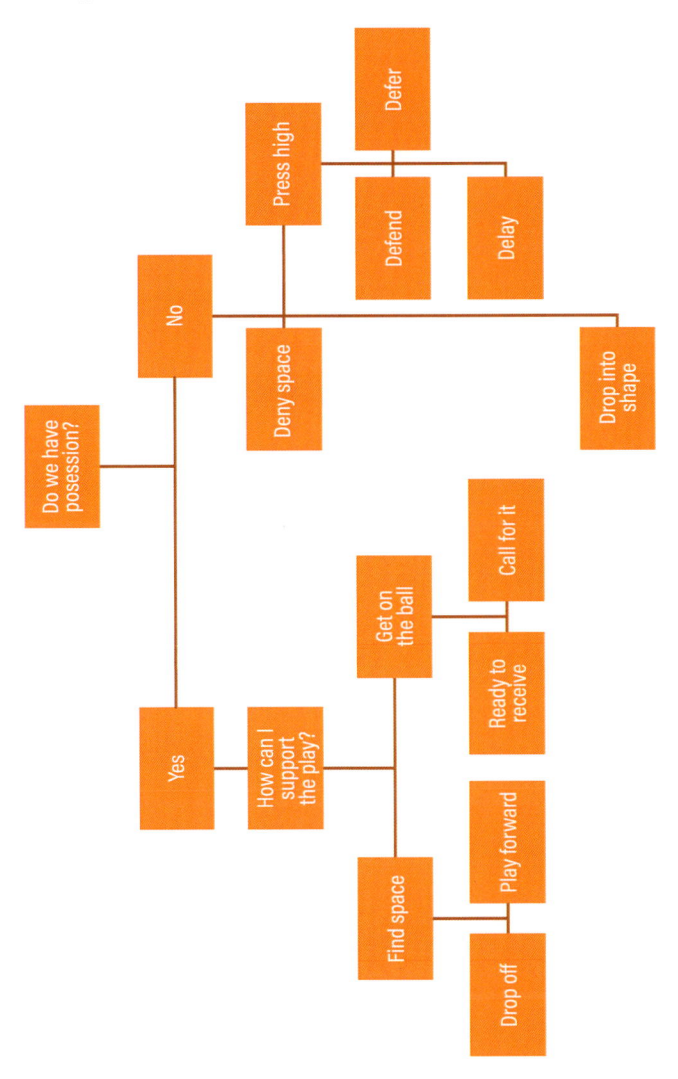

```
Do we have posession?
├── No
│   ├── Press high
│   │   ├── Defer
│   │   ├── Defend
│   │   └── Delay
│   ├── Deny space
│   └── Drop into shape
└── Yes
    └── How can I support the play?
        ├── Get on the ball
        │   ├── Call for it
        │   └── Ready to receive
        └── Find space
            ├── Play forward
            └── Drop off
```

One point of caution, as the young footballers get older, some may want to challenge your information given…. but isn't this good conversation and development?

One final part in this chapter is to share with you examples of communicating a clear strategy and vision for your team.

Again, these are just examples, but they are ones that I have used to good effect.

I have found this to be useful as:

- A continued point of reference
- Communication to players
- Communication to parents
- A recruitment tool
- Something to share with anyone else who may be interested

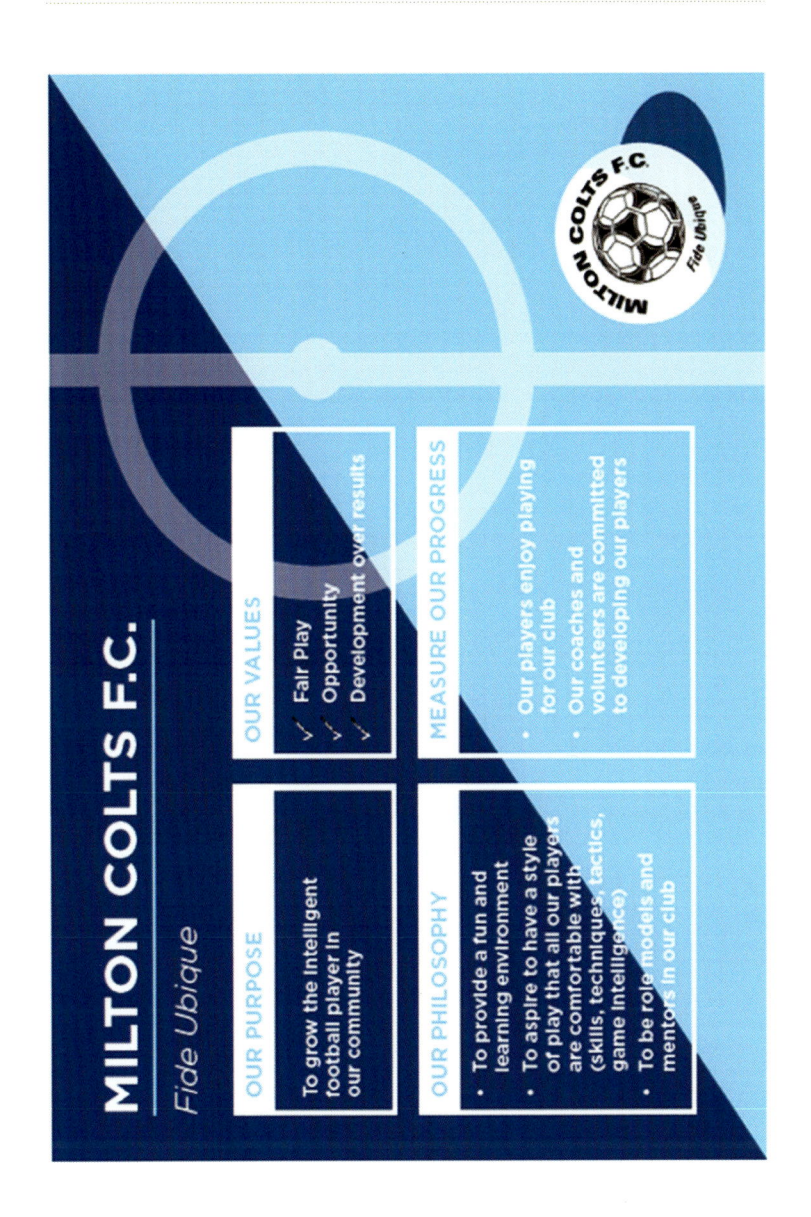

Chapter 6: Have a Clear Strategy and Vision for your Team

MILTON COLTS F.C.

Fide Ubique

OUR PURPOSE

To grow the intelligent football player in our community

OUR VALUES

- Fair Play
- Opportunity
- Development over results

OUR PHILOSOPHY

- To provide a fun and learning environment
- To aspire to have a style of play that all our players are comfortable with (skills, techniques, tactics, game intelligence)
- To be role models and mentors in our club

MEASURE OUR PROGRESS

- Our players enjoy playing for our club
- Our coaches and volunteers are committed to developing our players

Fide Ubique

Developing the Intelligent Young Footballer

Cambridge City U16 Strategy 2018 / 2019

Our Purpose

"To Develop the Intelligent Football Player"

Our Philosophy
(Our environment)

To play football at the highest level you enjoy

To prepare for the transition from U16 to U18 football

This Season

Maintain and enhance reputation as a football team

Be competitive

Be a better player

Develop the individual

Chapter 6: Have a Clear Strategy and Vision for your Team

In conclusion, of this chapter to set a clear strategy and vision for your team, I would recommend considering:

- **Development over results**
- **Set a vision and coach a style of play**
- **Active recruitment or develop what you have?**
- **Rotate or fixed positions?**
- **Equal or earned game time?**
- **What formation do you play through the age groups?**
- **Be transparent and open**
- **How is your team recognised by their style of play?**

Chapter 7: How do you Measure Success and Development?

How do you know that you are doing the right and best thing for your players? How do you measure success and progress?

One of the easiest ways to measure success is by the number of trophies that you win. It is great when you see young children winning the Cup or League. Talking to a friend recently he said that all he wanted to do as a young lad growing up was to get medals and win.

I get that, for many that is what they want but there is a reality that only one team can win the league each season and only one team can win the cup, unless of course it is the same team!

So, does that mean for all the other teams there has been no success and no development? I doubt it.

Whereas winning the Leagues and Cups is a great achievement and will create lifelong memories it is certainly not the only way to measure success. This of course can't be the measure in non-competitive football.

Ultimately it is about creating special childhood memories and experiences and here are some measures

Chapter 7: How do you Measure Success and Development?

that you can consider with the intent being that by the end of this chapter I have challenged you to create your own list:

- Fun. That all your players have fun and that they enjoy being in your environment. That they turn up every week engaged and connected wanting to be there. Development becomes so much easier when players are engaged and connected, they will play with a smile on their faces with energy and enthusiasm. If your players are having fun and enjoying it, you are probably feeling the same.
- Development. That you can see progress and improvement through the application. That an individual player has become better and improved aspects of their play and that the team has become stronger as a result. The pace of development will vary, for some it may be incremental for others it may be rapid. I like to ask the parents "has your child enjoyed it and have they improved since last season?". If the answer to both is yes, then job done for now. In a season I like to measure our results against teams we play. For example, if we lost the first game, how did we do in the return fixture? That can be seen as a form of team development.
- Retention. Do your players (and parents) want to stay with you and come back the next week or the next season? Players and parents generally won't stay anywhere where they are not enjoying it or not developing.

- Attract and recruit. Do players (and parents) want to join you and your club? A lot depends on if you are a club who actively recruits or are one who is more relaxed about it. The ability to attract and recruit players is generally a measure of your approach and the environment you create and your reputation.
- Offered Academy Trials or Contracts. I think it is great recognition if you have worked with a player, develop them, and they can then move onto bigger and better things in the game. At grassroots level one of these measures is any of your players being offered Academy trials or contracts. You must be doing something right. As much as it is great to keep your players and continue to develop them... I have never stood in the way of a player moving on and in fact I have encouraged it and have been very pleased for them and their family. These opportunities don't come around too often and as long as they want to, they have the desire and ambition, you have got to encourage them to take the opportunity and experience.
- Can they play in at least two positions? I think that it is important that players can play well and be both comfortable and competent in two different positions. This is great development. It challenges their appreciation of the game and amplifies their odds of continuing in the game after they leave you. Take this example, what if the player is a good wide right attacking player and that is their only preferred

Chapter 7: How do you Measure Success and Development?

position. What happens when teams get competitive and new and better players join and one is a wide right attacking player. It then becomes competitive for that one position. If the player in possession can't respond and keep their place, they may find their game time being restricted. However, if the player can say play wide left attacking or wide right defending, then they have more options for game time. The same applies when they eventually move on, which they will, what happens if they join a new team and can't get a game in their preferred position? They are then without game time until they can win the place in the team. We have a duty to develop players so that they are comfortable and competent in at least two positions.

- Continued learning and growth (of their ability). Have they won any of the end of season trophies? Have they won a 'Player of the Year', or 'Most Improved', as voted by their team mates and peers or by the coaching team (typical trophies presented)? Can you see that they are getting better as a player, they still want to listen, learn, take on information. It is our responsibility to develop all players whatever level they start at. As rewarding as the player heading off to the Academy, is the player progressing who some thought may be limited. Enjoy seeing all players develop and give the recognition and appreciation.
- Fulfil potential. We have all had players who were full of promise and potential at an early age both from

> "Trust is like the air we breathe. When it is present, nobody notices. But when it is absent, everybody notices"
>
> **Warren Buffet**

Chapter 7: How do you Measure Success and Development?

a technical and enjoyment perspective. Have you developed them in a way that they have fulfilled their potential? On many occasions we have seen players not fulfil their potential and I always personally take that as feedback. Why not, what could I have done differently? I have heard coaches take the easy way out and point the finger back and say it is down to the player, they didn't apply themselves. In some cases, it may be the case, but it is always a point I challenge and question my approach. These are young children and they only have one childhood to enjoy football.

- Dominate games. In attack and defence personally, I think it is great and a real measure of success and development when you see a team play with flair and enjoyment… but equally that they can drop into shape, understand their roles and responsibilities and dominate a game in and out of possession.

I love to see young children starting out in the game just running around, chasing every ball with energy and enthusiasm and playing with a smile on their faces.

We all know though that this is not sustainable long term and we eventually have to teach them and help them understand positions, roles and responsibilities in the game and within a team. Throughout and at all youth ages it is important to continue to let them have fun and enjoy the game. However, we are not just babysitters where we set up sessions just to let children run around and play. We are coaches with a clear responsibility to provide a fun environment, but also one where we coach and develop the players. Through the ages as tactics, formations and roles and responsibilities become more apparent, it is as rewarding for the coach and player when they get it and it happens in a game.

- Celebrate goals. In the early days we tend to see young children celebrating goals scored, because it is fun and for all there will be the first time they score a goal and that makes them happy. As the players get a bit older, they tend to stop doing it so much. Perhaps because it is a bit embarrassing or they just don't know how to, or the Coach doesn't encourage it. Personally, from about U12 on I like to strongly encourage teams to celebrate all goals scored. It is an achievement in a game and must have done something well to score. Celebrate it. It is recognition of progress, and it is fun. My line is to celebrate together. When a goal is scored, "go together" and celebrate. For me it creates:

  - A feel-good factor
  - It fosters team spirit and togetherness
  - A sense of belonging
  - A sense of achievement
  - An opportunity to have fun

Chapter 7: How do you Measure Success and Development?

Once encouraged a few times and the players see and feel the value, they do it without prompting and because they want to. At an U16 cup final when our team scored their third goal it sparked a favourite moment in football for me. The boys had celebrated the first and second, but the third was described by the Club Chairman as "the best celebration of a goal and togetherness", he had seen. Now I am sure the boys felt at 3-0 it was game over and they felt it was really time to celebrate, but it was truly a special moment for all players, coaches, parents and spectators to observe.

"If you do not celebrate success, you have none"

And finally, …

- To be able to say hello and goodbye with equal amounts of enthusiasm. Let's face it, all our players will leave us at some point. A good friend and respected coach recently had to say goodbye to all of his players, as he had come to the end of his time as a Youth Coach at U18, an emotional and poignant moment. Whatever reason it is that a player leaves you, I think a good measure is that they leave with a good opinion of you as a coach and that there is no animosity. This applies to both the player and the parent. We welcome players to our clubs with high levels of enthusiasm. Sometimes if players leave along the way they may end up coming back to you. You have to leave the door open for that opportunity.

How have the players who have left you and the club left? Was it with equal amounts of enthusiasm and respect? (whatever the reason)

So, how do you measure success and development? Write your own checklist but in general terms, here is mine to benchmark against.

- ☐ Your players have fun and enjoy being part of your environment
- ☐ That you can see and feel players developing and becoming intelligent young footballers
- ☐ Retention, that they want to stay and continue to be part of your team and environment
- ☐ Attract and recruit, that players want to join your team and set up and, in many cases, it will be about your reputation
- ☐ Player progression, that they have gone onto the next level, e.g., Academy contract. That you have developed them to this point in their journey
- ☐ Can they play in at least two different positions, have you given them the opportunity to learn the game from different perspectives?
- ☐ Continued learning and growth, that from whatever level they started, that they continue to learn, grow and be better
- ☐ Fulfil potential, that they progress as hoped and expected. Each player will eventually find their level,

Chapter 7: How do you Measure Success and Development?

and it is our job to help them find it and fulfil their potential.
- ☐ Dominate games in attack and defence. That you can see your players play their part in a team, playing and enjoying the beautiful game with both flair and discipline.
- ☐ Celebrate goals, the sense of achievement, belonging, togetherness, and to have fun and enjoy it. If you do not celebrate success, you have none
- ☐ Say hello and goodbye with equal amounts of enthusiasm. Do it well and with respect
- ☐ And finally, let's not ignore it, WINNING, but in the right way

Chapter 8: Be a Good Communicator and an Even Better Listener

This chapter is broken into two elements...

1. How to be a good communicator
2. How to be an even better listener

The real purpose of being a good or great communicator and an even better listener in developing the intelligent footballer is to be able to connect and engage, with the children and the parents and to help prepare the children for the future, both in and out of football.

At this point, I should also clarify that this is about face-to-face interaction and not using technology.

The world is rapidly changing, and we need to embrace technology to accelerate communicating but only where it will make us better. Do not replace face to face opportunities with technology just because you can.

I do use technology and my preference is to use What's App to communicate with parents but not the children. I know that a lot of young children from the age of 11/12

Chapter 8: Be a Good Communicator and an Even Better Listener

will have phones and communication with them could be easier and quicker.

However, we all know that we should not use technology to communicate with U18. Although it may be efficient and effective, to me it is fraught with concerns from a Safeguarding children perspective.

My stance is not to use it, and not to put myself or the club in to any difficult and unnecessary situation that can be avoided.

Use technology to communicate with parents, not any children U18.

Do you use technology to communicate direct to U18 players/children?

Being a good face to face communicator.

Based on my experience, recognising when communication has gone well but equally when it hasn't, here are my guiding principles to be a good communicator:

- Be clear, transparent, honest and authentic.

    In some cases, you may have to prepare what you are going to say, and this can be good practice as it helps you ensure that you get your message across. This is commonly used in preparing session plans or team talks. However, the majority of the time your communication will be "off the cuff" and you are reacting to situations as they happen. This doesn't mean that you can't build yourself some tactics to help you prepare. Personally, I like to take a breath and then prepare in my mind what I am going to say. I have seen other coaches do things like take a drink of water or walk to pick something up.

Taking a breath, based on my personal experience, I have found that to be a good tactic as in some cases in the heat of the moment I have not given myself the space and permission to pause and think about my message. What approach can you adopt to give yourself some brief but valuable thinking space and prepare yourself to communicate a good message.

Another tactic I like to use is the 'rule of three', as mentioned earlier. What are the three key messages that I want to get across. It helps me prepare my thoughts and it helps communicate the message in a concise way.

If your players and children get comfortable and familiar with you using the rule of three... you can always use it to test their listening and understanding. For example, "what are the three things we want to focus on in tonight's session?"

It is important for you to continue developing your communication skills.

Research has indicated that public speaking is one of the top four most stressful things for an adult alongside things like getting married, moving to a new house and bereavement. Every time you talk to your children or parents, you are public speaking to an

Chapter 8: Be a Good Communicator and an Even Better Listener

audience. Therefore, cut yourself some slack and give yourself time and permission to continue to learn and develop. Practice and you will get better at it, there will be a payoff including being more comfortable and reducing any anxiety that you may be feeling.

- Prepare when you can
- Breathe before talking
- Use the rule of three
- Being a good communicator for many is a learned behaviour, however, key stages are:
- To be clear with your message you want to communicate, plan it to reduce anxiety
- Be transparent, communicate often to engage and connect
- Be honest, and remember you are a volunteer and you want to develop, have fun and enjoy what you are doing
- Be authentic and be you

Ask questions.
Being a good coach is also about asking questions to inspire people to find their own solutions.

Asking questions is also a very important component of being a good communicator. Asking questions ensures that you have the opportunity to listen to understand and respond appropriately.

Asking questions also ensures engagement, because it encourages involvement and generally, someone will respond all be it in many cases the biggest characters in the group. Don't be afraid to use the power of silence though. Sometimes we ask questions and there are no responses. Hold the silence and nine times out of ten, someone will say something.

Asking questions allows you to engage with feedback and I am a great believer that if you surround yourself with feedback, you can only get better.

At a recent session I asked the players to give me feedback on the session. A few things were said but not too much. So, I then asked them all to give the session a mark out of 10, with 10 being the best it could be. All players gave feedback and it indicated what went well and what areas there were opportunities to improve. From a communication perspective, everyone was involved, and everyone had a voice which is very important if you want to create a safe, inclusive and trusting environment.

Have you ever asked your players to rate your session, on a scale of one to ten, and if so, what feedback did you receive, and what did you learn?

Asking questions demonstrates a vulnerability and builds trust in you that don't always have all the answers and in not always dictating and talking. It demonstrates you being open and that is always good for building relationships.

Chapter 8: Be a Good Communicator and an Even Better Listener

Asking questions demonstrates that you are prepared to listen and that you can then respond to help them assimilate and understand the information and to give them a response to what they have said, whether this is agreeing and validating or adding more to the story.

In your next session, what questions do you want to ask to create effective two-way communication through...

- **Appropriate responses**
- **Feedback**
- **Measurement**
- **Engagement**
- **Building relationships**
- **Vulnerability**
- **Listening**

Asking questions helps me check that my message has been understood and it also helps me articulate my thoughts and feelings.

Be an even better listener.

Based on my experience here are my guiding principles in being an even better listener.

You must create the space and permission to listen and to listen to understand and not just to reply or respond. If players and parents know that you, do it on a regular basis you will help them prepare to talk and open up dialogue.

For example, getting the players together at the end of the session or game allows them the space and permission to talk and for you to listen. Another practice that I adopt is to create the space to be approachable at the end of a session or game and it could be as simple as the time to walk back to the car. Being approachable is an important trait of being a good listener.

If you are not getting a lot of feedback or questions, ask for feedback and ask for responses to your questions and you will create the dialogue. The same applies to the parents. Creating the space and permission for them to air their views, thoughts and feelings is important.

Not all players and parents are comfortable talking in front of other people. This is a skill and attribute that you can help them with, develop over time, the more comfortable they get with you, the more they will start to trust the process and you.

For those who are not comfortable talking in front of others you still have to find a way to give them the space and permission.

Two approaches I take to this are:

- Offering to be available for a one-to one and being approachable to do so. Don't offer it and then never be approachable. If both players and parents see and feel it happening, they will begin to trust the process.

Chapter 8: Be a Good Communicator and an Even Better Listener

- Go specifically to a player or parent or both and ask questions or ask for feedback. This of course can be done with parents via email or WhatsApp etc, but I far prefer face to face. You can ask what you would like to find out and then pick up on the body language and tone of voice to ascertain what they are saying is authentic and real.

How often have you seen player and or parent say that they are enjoying it, but the body language doesn't project the same message?

How do you create the space and permission to listen for both players and parents?

Always listen to understand and not to reply. I have seen many coaches in the past listen but are ready to reply before they have fully listened. I have also seen many coaches get defensive when they feel challenged by questions and feedback. Taking the approach to listen to immediately reply in my opinion doesn't build trust and relationships and will eventually close conversation "because he doesn't listen, and he is not approachable".

I understand that you are volunteering your time and it can be unfair at times with all the challenge that you can get… but as a reality check… unfortunately, it goes with the territory of being the coach.

You are the 'leader' of the team and having 'your people' engaged, connected and happy is your responsibility. You create the environment and the zone and tone of the team. You may not have considered it in this way, but it is part of the role that you have signed up for.

At times I think it is expected that as coaches we have all the answers. We don't! You should recognise and appreciate this fact to help you engage with your players and parents. I learned this as part of my journey and I feel, and I feel that there is a lot of learning to be had in creating the right and best environment. I always want to provide the best environment that is safe, fun and for their development.

If you create the space and permission to talk and listen, in my experience it becomes an engaged, connected and appreciated environment.

If you surround yourself with feedback, you can only get better.

Take the feedback as a gift that will help you improve and be better. You have to not only receive the feedback; you have to accept it and then choose to do something with it. It may be that you change something to improve and be better, or it may be that you choose to ignore it. Either way you have made a choice. I would point out though that if you have heard similar feedback on a number of occasions, it may be worth taking action as there must be a theme emerging.

Chapter 8: Be a Good Communicator and an Even Better Listener

As you know, not all feedback is negative, although there is a stigma that it can be. We all secretly like it when we get positive feedback.

For me, there are two main types of feedback… constructive feedback with the intent to improve and be better and…appreciative feedback, recognition of valued achievements and contributions.

Creating the environment for dialogue gives you the opportunity to hear the feel-good feedback and the recognition and appreciation of what you are doing well as well as the potential opportunities to improve and be better. It is a win/win all round.

You have to demonstrate that you have listened and understood.

If you continue to create the space and do nothing with it then the feedback and questions will stop coming. In my opinion that is not a healthy and thriving environment. I really don't like it when you feel that parents are talking about you in a negative way and not with you to improve.

The conversation will still happen, but you won't hear it, and, in my experience, it is better to hear and understand than not.

You are trying to develop players and create the sense of belonging to a team and a purpose.

Don't close the interactions, encourage it and embrace it and see and feel the advantages long term.

I am not saying that you have to change everything that you will hear and understand. You still have to be the authentic 'leader' and be comfortable in your own skin, you still have to be you and you have to make your own decisions and choices.

If you can articulate your thinking behind your decisions and the reasons not to change, then people will still see that the process of listening is happening. "I have listened to your feedback and I have decided to ..." This works as people feel they have been listened to and they now know what is happening. They may not agree, but they understand. My experience also says that if they understand your thinking and perspective, it helps to align, and they can see what you see.

Encourage meaningful conflict.

Let me make this clear, I am not a fan of conflict, but I am if it is meaningful with an intent to find a better solution and improve.

Last night in a training session a young 12-year-old player challenged my instruction. Brilliant!

When young players are learning the game and start to have opinions, I think this is great and good players will challenge you as they get older.

It helps you develop their understanding and then when you see it being applied you have a great opportunity to give recognition and the learning has happened. It helps them embed their learning.

Chapter 8: Be a Good Communicator and an Even Better Listener

The example from the training session last night was that in a game a lot of one, twos in triangles were being played. Good, but my instructional challenge was to take the ball on the back foot and open up the play and not just to go back where they have come from.

"Why can't I play a one, two?"

"You can, but I know you can play one, twos, challenge yourself, to open your body and let me see if you can open up the play?"

Meaningful conflict because we had a good debate and involved the other players. By the end of the session a good number of them were opening their body and playing different and good passes. It felt good and they saw and felt the value of the new skill. Great development.

In summary, to be a great communicator:

- **Be clear, transparent, honest and authentic**
- **Give the space and permission**
- **Use the rule of three to communicate your message**
- **Continue to develop your approach**
- **Ask questions… and to be an even better listener:**

- **Give the space and permission**
- **Ask for feedback**
- **Be approachable**
- **Listen to understand**
- **Demonstrate and prove that you have listened**
- **Encourage and embrace meaningful conflict**

Being both an effective communicator and listener will engage both the children, the players and the parents… and will help prepare and develop the intelligent young footballers and for further education and prepare them for their careers whatever direction they take in the future.

Chapter 9: Help your Players with Education and Game Progression

How to Listen

Tilt your head slightly to one side and lift your eyebrows expectantly.
Ask questions.

Delve into the subject at hand or let things come randomly.
Don't expect answers.

Forget everything you've ever done. Make no comparisons. Simple listen

Listen with your eyes, as if the story you are hearing is happening right now.

Listen without blinking, as if a move might frighten the truth away forever.

This is your chance to listen carefully. Your whole life might depend on what you hear.

Joyce Sutpen

Chapter 9: Help your Players with Education and Game Progression (Beyond the Game)

As much as I love football and seeing young children play, I am also big on education. My wife has been a big influence on this and helping me understanding the importance.

Education is important throughout but no more so than when leading into GCSE and A Level year.

The children will never get his time again and their results could be life changing. We have a duty to ensure that the individuals have the right balance to enjoy the beautiful game but at the same time having a focus on their education.

At Cambridge City, as we moved into the U16 season I felt that it would be too disruptive to their study and revision to take two evenings out for training as it had been in previous seasons. With the travel to and from the training and then the session itself, it would be unlikely unless they were very dedicated that they would pick up

Chapter 9: Help your Players with Education and Game Progression

their books and get on with study and revision when they got home. We agreed to have one longer session per week and therefore they could have an extra evening in the week to study and revise.

At first it didn't go down particularly well with the players, but it did with the parents!

In addition, as the fixtures and games were on a Sunday, we could train on the Friday and at the end of their school week. It worked really well in shifting the mindset from the school week to the weekend and football.

The boys had a great football season with many special football memories and experiences and as a bonus, they also did well in their exams.

As a coach are you all about the football, or are you equally interested in their education?

Giving the time, space and permission to study and revise is important as it emphasises the importance and your actions in support of your commitment to them. It certainly helps engage the parents and is appreciated.

How do you support your young footballers with their education?

It is our role to understand and appreciate the impact of change that is going on in the lives of these young children both in their mindset and with their bodies as they grow and develop. Supporting them with education is very important as is…

Building in recovery periods as their bodies grow and not to overload. We have to be aware of other sporting and physical activities that they may be involved in such as a school's football programme, links to other development centres and elite squads and trying other sports, such as athletics, cricket and rugby. In addition, I have known of other activities such as dance and drama that adds to the demand on their young bodies.

I know we all think playing the beautiful game should be the priority, but there appears to be so many opportunities for young people to participate in now.

Understand their world and support them to be the best they can be. Challenge them but don't overload them and allow them to time to recover and stay in love with the game.

I have found that around the 12–14 age group there is a lot of physical and mental growth in the players and this places demand on their bodies.

My eldest son, in one calendar year grew seven inches. His body was in pain as his bones grew and his muscles were being stretched. With the amount of football, he had scheduled and expected to be present, there was no recovery time. He was struggling to get up and down the stairs in the house.

Chapter 9: Help your Players with Education and Game Progression

After his release from the Academy, we took him to a consultant and discovered that he had a serious back injury that was attributed to his demanding schedule. We were advised that if we didn't do something immediately, then there could be long term implications.

The consultation mandated that he had to do 10 weeks of absolute no physical activity. Imagine that for a young lad from a physical and mental wellbeing perspective, no sport...

However, it was absolutely the right and best thing to do as he did recover and worked his way back to fitness and to play at a good level of football and performance. It was a massive learning curve for me. I was the parent that encouraged him to continue playing and training "you will be fine" without any real appreciation of what was going on in his body. I vowed that I would never let this happen again with my youngest son and anyone who I have the privilege to coach. I will build in recovery time and never force anyone to play.

Young footballers should not be expected to be present and carry on playing throughout significant growth periods.

As a coach now in the modern world we have to get the balance right in encouraging players to play but at the same time helping them perform the best they can. If they are not fit, they can't perform, and this has a knock-on impact on their enjoyment.

In some cases, this may mean giving your children the time and permission not to play and allow for pain free growth. You have to help them grow into their adult bodies.

How do you recognise and look after your players as they grow and in particular if they talk to you about injuries and pain?

Another key factor in supporting young children being able to perform to the best of their ability is to educate on nutrition and sleep.

In the world of fast foods, it is easy to access food that are treats and enjoyable to eat. In my opinion, that is ok in moderation. However, we should play a part in educating what foods and drinks are best and in particular for pre and post training and pre and post on match days.

I am not a nutritionist, but I have accessed information to share with players and parents to help them learn about the benefits to feel better and prepared to perform and enjoy. It helps them understand the importance pre and post training and on match days. I have seen benefits and in the coming season this is something that I want to develop further with the players and parents alike.

There is a lot of general and generic information available on the web and anyone can access it. However, making it more specific for pre and post training and games does help the understanding of what to do and when.

Chapter 9: Help your Players with Education and Game Progression

What interest do you take in educating your children/players to understand nutrition and sleep?

We can't mandate this at grassroots level, but we have a duty to at least challenge the mindsets and preconceived ideas. Engaging with the parents is equally important as in most cases it will be them who provide the food and manage the sleep patterns.

Appreciate and understand them and let them still be children.

I have observed a large spectrum of approaches by coaches and there is a continuum for grassroots coaches.

Where do you sit in the continuum?

All about fun ———————————————— **Aspiring Academy Level**

I believe that in the first instance we all have a duty to create a fun and learning environment. We have to allow the children to have fun, their first memories and experiences of football has to be fun and let them fall in love with the game. 100% of children should have fun at football.

In a recent conversation I had with someone from the PFA, he said, "football and fun in the same sentence, you don't often hear that these days" Let's face it, if young children do not first fall in love with the game, then they won't develop and perhaps excel.

For that reason, certainly in the early stages, it should be all about fun…No one ever excelled at anything without first falling in love with it.

I remember watching a U16 game and one team turned up super prepared and very serious. They obviously had a very committed set of coaches and players.

The other in contrast were probably there for the social aspect and friendship. Their warm up consisted of just smashing balls around and having a laugh and joke. There was no intervention from the coach until had to get them in together and pick 11 to start.

Which approach was right and wrong?

I got talking to one of the parents whose son was playing for the competitive team. They clearly had a set of talented boys, very focussed and committed. He said, "sometimes I wish my lad played for a team like the others. They only want to be there because they want to, and they clearly enjoy it".

Interesting observation, I didn't ask if his son wasn't enjoying his football!

So where does the fun stop… it shouldn't. For me it is all about creating the best memories and experiences that we can and where we can facilitate young footballers to be the best they can be.

Chapter 9: Help your Players with Education and Game Progression

Young footballers should be able to play at the highest level they can for as long as they can that they enjoy.

At a training session with a set of U13 lads recently, although it was focussed and engaging... I heard two lads talking about eating dog tails!!! Priceless, the curious and imaginative mind of a 12-year-old! Young boys just being young boys. We need to create an environment of discipline and respect, but we also need to create an environment where they can have fun, be friends, be children and talk about things like FIFA and Minecraft or whatever the latest game or fad is...

Let them have fun and have fun with them.

Help them become confident and comfortable in the company of adults. We have a role to play in helping young children be confident in communicating with people at all levels.

Many children will see us coaches as being scary people. Unapproachable, very focussed, disciplined, too loud and intimidating. Outside their families and school teachers, we could be their first and maybe their only interaction with an adult.

As they grow through their lives, whether it be in sport or in business, effective interaction with people is important and necessary, and if we can help them develop through our approach then great.

It is a life skill we are helping them develop and the importance resonated with me when a parent said to me:

"Not only in his football development, I have been really impressed with how he has developed in his confidence in talking to adults".

To be honest, I hadn't realised to that point that I was having that impact. Since then, I have made it part of my purpose in developing the intelligent young footballer.

Build relationships with them. Be approachable, be authentic and be honest.

Be generous in the fact that you should love and enjoy seeing other people succeed.

As a football coach we have one of the real privileges and luxuries in life... we have the ability to positively impact people's lives. We can influence and inspire. That is a big responsibility but ultimately a privilege.

It goes back to the purpose of why you do it and so I will ask the question again for you to reflect on:

Is it all about you and the trophies that you win, or is it really all about developing the intelligent young footballer, and creating unique and special memories and experiences?

We have a duty to do it the right way to treat both the children and the parents with respect and care.

Chapter 9: Help your Players with Education and Game Progression

If you have a set of players to work with, work with them. Be interested in them as individuals as well as being part of a team.

Ask them and take genuine interest about their families, their holidays, their favourite teams, their school work...

Here is something that can help you be the best leader you can be... challenge yourself to know at least three things (here is the 'rule of three' again) about every child/player in your team beyond the football. Build the relationship and make time to be interested. Don't pay lip service to it, these young footballers will see that.

I know that all coaches are not comfortable with this but sometimes we have to challenge ourselves to be better and move out of our comfort zones.

Can you visualise the coach who?

- Doesn't engage with his players and parents?
- Is all about the football and not interested in anything else?
Lives by the results and performances?

If you can, what reputation do they have?

Flip that and you can now visualise the coach who:

- Does engage
- Is interested in developing the whole person
- Is successful but is not all about the results

What reputation do they have as a coach?

Reflect... what about you, where do you think your players, parents and other coaches would position you?

Let your children and their parents know that you are there for them at all times. Be a leader and mentor.

As a coach we have to give instruction and guidance, we are after all helping them to learn and understand.

The majority of the time we will do it in a group situation. However, we must always make ourselves available for individual conversations to help develop not only the team but the individual.

What balance of your time do you spend with the team, the group vs time with the individual players?

My conclusions in helping players with their education and game progression beyond the beautiful game are:

- **Demonstrate your commitment to their education**

- **Build in recovery periods**

- **Educate on nutrition and sleep**

Chapter 9: Help your Players with Education and Game Progression

- **Let the children be children, it has to be fun and have fun with them**
- **Help them be confident with adults**
- **Be interested in them as individuals beyond the football**
- **Be there for them**

Chapter 10: Influential and inspirational quotes

I love a quote and I am always looking out for a quote to influence or inspire my thinking. If a quote makes me stop and think, then it is worth recording and referring to every now and again. If it accelerates my learning into taking action and doing something even better. You will have seen throughout the book that I have included quotes that have resonated with me and here are others too good and impactful for me to be left out my book.

I hope that these quotes in some way influence and inspire you...

"Nobody told me how to control a ball or pass a ball. Most of my ability came from experimentation with the ball. There are coaches nowadays who weren't good enough to play insisting on coaching things footballers don't need to be coached on. Too many coaches making the game about themselves rather than the kids".
Gordon Strachan

"Kids do not feel sad for losing, they feel sad when they think the coach doesn't love them or appreciate them".
Pep Guardiola

Chapter 10: Influential and inspirational quotes

"If your actions inspire others to dream more, learn more and become more then you are a leader".
Quincy Adams

"Be the best you can be and have fun doing it and create something you are proud of".
Richard Branson

Johan Cruyff's last instruction to his players before they stepped onto the pitch for the 1992 European Cup Final. *"Go out and enjoy it."* The course of Barcelona's history changed forever.

"A trophy gathers dust. Memories last forever.".
Mary Lou Retton

"Without the ball, you can't win".
Johan Cruyff

"He who does not want to win has already lost".
Unknown

"Intelligent players always understand that the real star is the team and what they give to the team and what the team gives back to them".
Arsene Wenger

"It was becoming apparent to me that to succeed one must master one's profession".
Montgomery, India 1909

"There is no disgrace in wanting to win, but it has to be done the right way within the spirit of football".
Arsene Wenger

"We don't just coach football. we coach decision making, we coach choices, we coach consequences, we coach respect. We coach life on and off the pitch".
Unknown

"I'm very much about the environment. If you can create the right one, 99.9% of people will improve".
Brendan Rogers

"The only things that ever get done are through people".
Unknown

"It is not where you start it is where you finish".
Ian Gillian

"The beautiful thing about learning is that no one can take it away from you".
B.B. King

"In the beginner's mind there are many possibilities, but in the expert's mind there are few".
Shunnya Suzuki

"Leadership is about making others better as a result of your presence and making sure that the impact lasts in your absence".
Sheryl Sandberg, CEO of Facebook

Chapter 10: Influential and inspirational quotes

"If you always do what you've always done, you'll always get what you've always got".
Henry Ford, Industrialist

"No one cares how much you know, until they know how much you care".
Theodore Roosevelt, U.S. President

"People may hear your words, but they feel your attitude".
John C Maxwell, Author

"We do not remember days, we remember moments".
Cesare Paveses, Italian Poet

"I never teach my pupils. I only attempt to provide the conditions in which they can learn".
Albert Einstein, theoretical Physicist

"You miss 100% of the shots that you don't take".
Wayne Gretzky

"Leadership is not about titles, positions or flowcharts. It is about one life influencing another".
John C. Maxwell, Author

"Most people do not listen with the intent to understand; most people listen with the intent to reply".
Steven Covey, Author

"Finding your space on any team is all about making yourself selectable".
Gareth Southgate

"When I was growing up, the cultural reference points that defined your character were music, clothes and football".
Paul Weller, Musician

"You were born to win, but to be a winner, you must plan to win, prepare to win and expect to win".
Zig Zigler, Multicultural Speaker

"Spend 80% of your time focusing on the opportunities of tomorrow rather than the problems of yesterday".
Brian Tracy, Motivational Speaker

Chapter 11: Respected Coaches

I love to watch and observe and learn from other coaches. If you are similar to me and like to do the same, it really is great development and permission to reflect on what you do and how you compare.

Over my time as a grassroots coach, I have had the privilege and pleasure to work with some great coaches that I admire and respect. You have heard my story and now in this chapter it is an opportunity to include some of their wisdom and experience to help to continue to challenge and or validate your thinking.

I asked them to contribute to this book with their three top tips for Developing the Intelligent Young Footballer.

Thank you and appreciation to every one of you and I look forward to learning more from and with you as we continue with our privileged journey in developing the intelligent young footballers and creating some great memories and experiences along the way.

Robert Simpson, Glentaner Community Club, Aberdeen.

Enjoy it, commit to it and respect other coaches and your team mates.

Andrew Adams, Cambridge City Youth

Respect them, don't overcomplicate things and allow them to be themselves particularly U16 and younger.

Chris Wilkinson, Cambridge City Youth

Believe in yourself and encourage the players around you as these players will help you improve. Create the environment to allow as much practice as possible and get the players to work on and improve their first touch with both feet and their ability to carry the ball at speed with both feet. Get them to be comfortable with the ball. Encourage them to always make space to be available and look to be on the ball as much as they can.

Lindsay Bartlet, Glentaner Community Club, Aberdeen

Discipline, ensure that skills are carried out correctly, not just how they want to carry them out and in particular with regards to listening and time keeping. Consistency and encouragement always.

Dave Christie, Lifelong Friend, and Football Mentor

Develop their quick decision making and their ability to find space at the right moment. Let them practice, practice, practice and encourage deceptive tricks and moves and

Chapter 11: Respected Coaches

this will help them with their quick decision making and finding space at the right time. If you have confidence and composure and all of the above, then practice, practice, practice more.

Dallas Lawrence, Cambridge City Youth

Make the environment as awesome as it can possibly be, make it a sanctuary and a fortress. Be true to yourself and your belief. Don't be afraid to change your mindset, be open to other ideas from the players and coaches and be reactive to problems.

Ray Muirhead,
Dyce Boys Club, Aberdeen

Technique. In my opinion all the great players who were intelligent also had good technical ability…players that could move a pass quickly with one touch or a spin on a sixpence getting themselves out of trouble.

Knowledge. Teaching them how to make key/good decisions…doing this individually as a defender's decision making is different from say a forward or a winger.

Dedication. For all the intelligence a young player can have, if they don't have the dedication to want to succeed as a top player and work hard at it then they won't succeed…many young lads who have been intelligent skilful players have not had the dedication or the will to work hard and it can fall by the wayside.

Darren Lee, Milton Colts, Cambridge

Make it fun.

At grassroots level the coach's top priority is to make football fun and inclusive. Children will learn better and faster if they are enjoying what they are doing. Furthermore, they will keep playing football for longer if they continue to enjoy it.

Keep it real.

Training sessions should focus on maximum playing time and keeping the ball moving. When focusing on a particular element of the game, the training session needs to be designed so that it is quick and easy to explain and game related. The best training sessions simulate game scenarios, so that grassroots footballers can quickly and easily relate to the training session when they are playing matches and thus hopefully implement what they have learnt at the previous training session. Some of the best training sessions are played at high tempo and with real pressure, similar to game conditions. A grassroots coach should design a training session with the objective in mind of all the players being able to understand the purpose of the session and then being given the opportunity to implement it in a real match with great effect.

Chapter 11: Respected Coaches

Provide opportunity.

The best way to learn how to do something well is to do it and keep doing it; after time you will see improvement That improvement will continue the longer you stay at it. The more football grassroots players play and enjoy the more they will learn and continue to learn the game and develop into an intelligent footballer. Football is a team game will eleven players, as such, provide opportunity for all grassroots players to experience playing in all 11 positions on the pitch and continually rotate players rather than encourage them to focus on one position. This does, however, need to be balanced with the "top tip" of "making it fun". If a player really does not want to play in a particular position, then how you rotate that player around the various positions to help their development may need to be tempered so that it increases their enjoyment rather than undermine it.

Ian Gillan, Director of Football, Kedah

These are a few of my thoughts on grassroots football and some observations over my football journey.

Growing up in the Sunnybank (Aberdeen), close to several council housing areas, Powis, Froghall, The Gallowgate, Tillydrone etc. I attended the local schools and still have lifelong friends from those days. The schools attracted a variety of children from all different backgrounds. I started my education at Sunnybank Primary, then the institution of life Powis Academy. As you can imagine it was a diverse community consisting of the good, bad, the ugly and really ugly. Everyone has their own version and experiences from attending Powis Academy. Many graduated through the education system of the time, obtaining the ultimate award "The Certificate of Life".

    I sincerely believe that having not been part of this I wouldn't be the same person I am today. The school system was a real education and certainly gave life skills that are with me every day.

Self-Discovery: The game is the educator.

The coaching we had as kids was more of a self-discovery phase added with a little experience from the older kids or players. I remember getting kicked around by the older boys in the Sunnybank Park and in games. My turn came around when I matured. Today's coaching, I feel is too sterile and everything has to be perfect for them to train and play. Junior players are developing and don't need to be treated like professionals. Street football was a great educational tool in my time and all the kids in the area loved to play. The park was sometimes full of players from all the surrounding houses. Everyone enjoyed the games and it was an unconscious learning environment. This needs to be introduced in a modern format and futsal or 5-a-side etc. could be the answer?

Chapter 11: Respected Coaches

More casual gatherings of players and parents could be very good in the development, Self-discovery phase. Let the kids play and no coaching sometimes is better in this phase.

Squad Sizes: Game time needed for development.

The playing squad sizes today are too big. This limits the minutes of play on the weekend of each player. Everyone has to play and not playing isn't good for anyone. The game is the educator and if the coach or management are not so good in the coaching area the game as mentioned prior is important as the educator of the team and individuals. The more games the more football actions and you learn from the good and the bad.

Fun: Everyone enjoys himself or herself.

The objective of the game is to win but more importantly grassroots football is about having a good time. Winning is more enjoyable than getting beat but this again is all part of the process of creating better people not just football players. It is important to get positives out of every training session. As a coach, I believe you are trying to create an unconscious learning environment. Some players need strict discipline and others have self-control etc. At the end of the day its football, it can be 3v3, 8v9 as long as everyone is enjoying themselves and getting something out of the game at the "GRASSROOTS" level. Football is the winner and the players and coaches will return week in week out, rain, snow or sunny.

Technology: Good for Developing Technique

The new modern coaching applications for smart phones and Android are extremely useful. In this time of COVID-19 it is possibly the best way to train as no social distancing etc. required at home. The players also can practice using the smart phones and replicate the football actions. If they don't understand the exercise, they just need to reply the instance or section of the session. This can be extremely useful to the shy players both boys and girls. They can practice as much as they like, having a ball to themselves gaining confidence on and off the ball. More ball contact time is important to all players young or older. Confidence is the key to all the football actions and phases of play in the game.

I hope these little notes are of some kind of value and useful to yourself or others in your book. We had a great time playing football in the local park and garages etc. Now unfortunately it will be a thing of the past and possibly never to be seen again.

Chapter 12: Feedback from Children

Following on from the previous chapter and the thoughts and reflections from the experienced grassroots coaches that I have worked with that I have admired and respected, now is time to listen to and understand the perspectives of the children that we coach.

I asked children, both boys and girls with an age range of 7 to 18 what they want from a football coach. It makes very interesting reading and provides thought-provoking reflection.

What do the children, the young footballers you coach want from you as a coach?

If you are brave enough to take the time to ask the children that you coach, I am sure that you will find it very rewarding recognising what you do well and what they appreciate about your approach…you will also understand opportunities for you to potentially grow, develop and be better.

If you surround yourself with feedback, you can only get better.

Here are contributions of 21 children. Thank you.

Age 14, I think a coach needs to be enthusiastic, have strategic ability and be able to banter with the players.

Aged U14 years, three requirements that I feel is needed from a football coach is that they help me enjoy the game and develop. They have a very good understanding of the game, a good sense of humour and supportive of the team and individuals.

Aged 11 years, I want them to always be on time, enthusiastic and someone to help me grow and develop as a footballer.

Aged U13, they must have passion, ability to understand each player and communicates clearly.

Aged U18, from my experience and the many coaches that I have had…they create a relaxed atmosphere, welcomes feedback from players and communicates well.

Aged 13, I think they should have good relationships with the players and parents, take time to know the players weaknesses and strengths and makes sessions and training enjoyable.

Aged U13, I like coaches to be honest and help me drive myself to develop as a player and for them to give me

Chapter 12: Feedback from Children

feedback on what I need to work on and what worked well in training / games.

Aged 8 (girl) a happy and smiling coach, somebody who will control the naughty ones (those not listening or playing fair) and they make it fun!

Aged 12, letting us play practice games, it gives us time to practice our skills, our pace and our intelligence in the game. When coaches are trying to teach us something, they should show a video of when professionals do it, teach us the professionals' correct technique, it will help children to develop more and make harder skills easier.

Aged 13, a good coach gives me game time and lets me play. They give me instruction to help and don't just tell me to work harder, I am working as hard as I can. Stick with me, help me when things are not going so well for me.

Aged 12 (girl) I need a coach to be patient and help us learn new skills in different ways, to give us different activities, just not kicking a ball. To inspire me to reach my goals in football and really pushes us.

Aged 8, I want a coach to help me learn about football and learn new skills. They are an inspiration. That they show me how to be fair, pay attention, actually pay attention to every single one of us.

Aged 7, that the coach is nice, is the best, supports us, looks after my family (my brother and sister) and I have fun. I need them to be fierce to be exciting.

Aged U13, encourages you, doesn't shout at you or criticises you but gives you advice how to be better. Gives one to one advice, can give you advice on what to improve on and listens to what you say. Gives players opportunity, gives players the chance to play in positions that they think they could play well in and gives players time on the pitch.
Brothers aged 8 and 10, the coach needs to be happy and be fair and give the ball to everyone.

Aged 14, I need the coach to be supporting, kind and make it challenging but not too hard.

Aged 14.
Understanding the individual – it's important for a coach to understand an individual's strengths and weaknesses to be able to push a player to play to the best of their abilities. A coach needs to have a good understanding of a player's style of play and where they play best. If a player is coached in a way that doesn't suit their style of play, then it can ruin their performances. If you are coached to improve

your weaknesses and get better on things, you're not so strong on, then you will start to see massive improvements in your all-round play.

Encouragement – the last thing you want after losing a game is for your coaches to be going on about how the team didn't play well enough and picking on individual errors. Instead focusing on what you did well and then giving ways of correcting what didn't go so well is a much better way of improving the teams and the individual performances. It is also important that during a game, if an individual or the team do something really well, that the coaches praise them for this. This boosts confidence and can help the performance.

Playing the right way – I think a rather large part of a player's enjoyment for football, is through the style of play of their team. Quick passing football and scoring good team goals is much more enjoyable than playing the ball long and getting scrappy goals. If a coach encourages a player to be confident on the ball and to express themselves, it's more enjoyable and stress free, not having to constantly worry about making a mistake.

Aged 13, the top three things I need from a football coach that helps me enjoy the game and develop

Make training sessions enjoyable with teammates.

One of the most enjoyable things about football is spending time with friends/teammates. The coach needs to make training sessions fun for the players but not disruptive with players messing around. It really important for the coach to encourage and promote healthy relationships between teammates. When there are conflicts between players the coach needs to resolve them at the training session so that no players leave training with unresolved ill feelings with other teammates.

Make it special – Tours, tournaments.

Another good way to boost morale and increase enjoyment is to go on tours. Tours are lots of fun and they are a really good way to stay close as a team. As well as this on tours you get a ton of new experiences and get to see different playing styles and training techniques that you can take away. Lastly, it's a good way to relax and generally have a good time.

Tournaments are a good way to get touches on the ball, this is because the games are played on small pitches and played at a fast pace; they are also short, generally approx. 10 minutes, meaning time is of the essence to create your opportunities to perform well. During the group stages you quickly learn that if you lose a game there is always a way of coming back and getting a second chance but during the knock-out rounds its sudden death. It is a great feeling if you win as it is a brilliant accomplishment – especially if the road to victory has been a tough one; it shows you anything is possible even if at times it seems bleak. Tournaments are hugely competitive, so they can help to create a winning

Chapter 12: Feedback from Children

mentality. This will help you in your cup and league games which are just as competitive – if not more.

Thought through training sessions.

This is where the players come away with something they have learned and knowledge that will benefit their ongoing development. Some of my favourite training sessions are the ones which make me proud of myself because I know I have put a shift in and I know I put 100% into it; this experience is most enjoyable and effective when all the players are putting in 100% as well. Provided that the coach makes the training, sessions structured and easy for young players to relate to a match then I believe players are more likely to respect and understand that and they should then do their part.

Aged 14, I want the coach to set the bar high and expectations high in terms of long-term goals for me personally and for the team and for the standards of behaviour and respect although not necessarily expecting them to be achieved overnight. I also want the coach to encourage me to make my own decisions on the pitch and to develop good decision-making ability when under pressure. I want them to generate an excellent squad and team mentality, inclusive, mutually encouraging, supportive, welcoming and fun for everyone. There is no I in team kind of thing.

Aged 18, I want the coach to be credible, to know what they are on about and what they are saying will help me develop and be better. They also need to have a good social side that I can relate to and enjoy their company but at the same time, they need to make things happen and get done. It has to be fun with good variety. The best coaches that I have worked with are the ones that made it fun and enjoyable and the ones who have helped me develop as a footballer and as a person.

On reading this, what resonated with you?

Take this time to recognise and appreciate what you do well and equally take this time to think about the potential opportunities you have to grow and be better and to create the environment for young children to enjoy the beautiful game and to grow and develop.

Chapter 13: Celebrating Learning with and From Children

Over the last few months I have had the privilege and pleasure to learn with and from children in my role as a Director and Head Coach with the Football Fun Factory.

I have significant business experience and expertise in Leadership and People Development. However, I do give myself the permission to pause and reflect. How do you get the best and most out of your people…and in this case the children because they will tell you:

Here is my in…

1. **Always be prepared to provide the best environment, give them your best and they will give it back**

2. **You have to be thoughtful with the use of words and by your actions**

3. **Manners matter**

4. **You must always be approachable**

5. **Listen to understand and surround yourself with their feedback... if you do, you can only get better**

6. **Recognise and acknowledge what they do well**

7. **Enjoy it and celebrate success, if you do not celebrate success...you have none.**

Makes sense in engaging and connecting with people, but as adults, do we unlearn this somehow?

Chapter 14: Continue to Develop Yourself

Our world that we live in is ever changing and evolving as is the world of football.

I love to recall the glory days, my great memories and experiences of football growing up as I am sure you do.

We have to respect the past and see the future and if we are going to have a big part to play in developing the intelligent young footballers for the future... we have to continually develop ourselves.

This KEY:

Keep
Educating
Yourself,

and so, in this chapter we will explore what has changed, and will continue to change, how we need to continue to learn and develop and be the best we can be. As coaches and individuals, we are all different and therefore our development plans will be different based on our personal experiences and opportunities that we may have. For that reason, what we discuss in this chapter will hopefully inspire you to create your own personal development plan. It is KEY to your future success.

What is in your current personal development plan? Or how have you developed in the last year?

In your experience, what has changed in football and particular in relation to being at grassroots football?

Many coaches will already be very proud of what they do and what they have achieved. It is important to give yourself the permission to pause, for you to take time to reflect on what you have done and achieved.

I believe that we should never stop learning and developing and in relation to grassroots football here is what I think based on my experiences what has changed and will continue to change.

The expectations on the coach have increased.

Parents, children, players, officials from within in your club structure, League and FA officials all expect more and although we love this job... it could be close on 24/7 role with our responsibilities increasing both on and off the pitch.

For players and children, it is not only now about putting the team on the pitch to play. We now need to understand

Chapter 14: Continue to Develop Yourself

individual development as well as team dynamics and we need to provide clear direction and appropriate challenge. We must never forget that it has to be fun. We want them to fall in love and stay in love with the beautiful game. Therefore, there is an expectation to be good at building relationships. For player development it is not just about picking a team and the best players. It is about developing all your players / children with a focus on:

- Technical
- Tactical
- Physical
- Lifestyle

All our children are people first and players second, and we need to recognise and appreciate how they learn best that will definitely have an impact and influence on how they:

- Think
- Feel
- Behave

You create the environment and if your players are engaged, connected, learning and developing and behaving well… then you must be doing something right and embracing the challenges of a modern coach.

"Better coaches, better players, better football"
Ian Gillan

I have seen a shift over the years that more parents will stay and watch every training session as well as games. In some cases, this can be the mother, father or both and in some cases, it may be grandparents.

Every training session and every game we are putting on is a 'show' and we are being watched and observed by our actions and language. This has been a big learning curve for me in how I behave in and around all players.

The expectation from parents I think is that we provide the environment for their children to:

- ✓ Be safe
- ✓ Have fun
- ✓ Develop

Parents see how we talk to their children and they can also observe and watch our body language.

Parents will encourage their children to stay with you and your team if they feel all three of the above are being achieved. If not, then they may make the choice to move on.

Parents also expect you to be an effective communicator, approachable and honest. They are trusting you with the development and wellbeing of their child.

Over the years I feel as coaches we have had to develop our people management skills, build relationships and present and articulate with impact and clarity.

Chapter 14: Continue to Develop Yourself

We have had to accept being more open to receiving and accepting feedback and taking appropriate actions to improve and to be better.

The advent of technology to communicate has helped with efficient, quick and consistent communication and we all need to embrace technology.

To be an effective communicator and listener we have had to develop our approach to face to face communications and the understanding and application of technology whether it be one to one or in group situations.

Many years ago, when I was running an adults team, it was almost a one man show... but not anymore, the expectations have changed, and you may have a number of other coaches to support you, administrative support and a committee within the bigger club.

I would imagine most of you in running a youth team are part of a bigger club structure.

With that comes:

- Committee meetings
- Club guidelines and policies to be adhered to
- Manager meetings
- Annual club events and fundraisers

For all involved in a bigger club, if you want to represent the club and the brand you will have had to learn how to operate in these different environments and way beyond the field of play. I always find it intriguing to work with people with different backgrounds and different motives and the challenges of trying to gain alignment and buy into club ethos and policies.

For the old school coaches there will be many pros and cons to this approach, but it is a reality and expectation in our new world.

The likelihood is that for all teams there will be at least two coaches involved in providing the environment for children to enjoy the game. It some cases may be more. As well as this being a priority for safeguarding, it is a positive opportunity for different voices to play a part in the player and child development.

Great coaching relationships, aligned thinking and approach is a very positive structure to have in a team and can only be of benefit. This does not happen overnight and in some cases, it can be challenging if there is a conflict of views and opinions. A great coaching team will work this out over a period of time although for some, if alignment can't be achieved, then this may mean a separation and the pursuit of personal football ambitions. Healthy and meaningful conflict is ok, a toxic environment for the children is not.

As a coach we have to understand the dynamics of working with and in an effective coaching team.

Another big change is the amount of paperwork, paper based or electronic that we now have to complete either for our Club or League affiliations.

Chapter 14: Continue to Develop Yourself

I have made many mistakes with incomplete or late forms...and then incurred fines!! I just want to be a football coach, but the reality is that there will be a lot of admin to do for the successful operation of your team. Included in this is the collecting of subs and monies due, sponsorship and paying of pitch hire, referees, purchase of equipment including kit... understanding the finances management, is another developmental need.

We all need to be qualified as coaches now, to a minimum of the equivalent of Level One which includes safeguarding, DBS and First Aid. We all have to commit to the learning programmes to gain our licences and the continued professional development and refreshers to maintain these. Although a challenge for many, it is the right and proper thing to do to raise the standards and maintain compliance but above all to understand what is needed in our evolving world to provide a safe, fun and development environment for the children.

What cannot be underestimated, is the time, challenge and commitment involved. It is not always understood by the parents, but it is a requirement and licence to be able to undertake the tasks and duties of a football coach.

If you are reading this and you are thinking of starting this journey as a coach, you may feel slightly put off.

It is all very challenging with all the things we need to do, but it is ultimately a pleasure and privilege to be able

> "The greatest leader is not necessarily the one who does the greatest things. He/she is the one that gets the people to do the greatest things."
>
> **Ronald Reagan**

Chapter 14: Continue to Develop Yourself

to develop intelligent young footballers... Is it worth it? ... Absolutely 100%.

So as the world of football continues to evolve and change, what are the things that you should consider to Keep Educating Yourself?

- ☐ Be appropriated, qualified and have the coaching licences
- ☐ Understand the modern game, the changing tactics, techniques, physical and lifestyle demands
- ☐ Be a people manager and leader;
  - ◉ Build relationships
  - ◉ Develop people and teams
  - ◉ Be authentic
  - ◉ Make decisions
  - ◉ Deliver hard news with empathy (individual)
- ☐ Develop the individual, be great at having development conversations
- ☐ Be a good coach, develop your approach to coaching beyond just giving instruction
- ☐ Create an environment of engagement and connection to your strategy and vision, develop purpose and meaning
- ☐ Present with impact. Be a great communicator and listener, both face to face and embracing technology
- ☐ Develop your administration skills

☐ Be interested in the whole person and their wellbeing and development

This list is not exhaustive, you can add you own based on your experience. It is intended as both a skills audit and to provoke thought on your personal development.

I have seen some technology savvy coaches start to film games and to collect data on speed and agility. This is something that will become more accessible and expected particularly as players get older. It will be on my future development plan to be able to understand and collect data and to do analysis to aid development and performance.

What else can you to do to continue to develop?

- Read books and watch videos
- Observe and watch other coaches and pundits. At grassroots I watch coaches at every game I go to. I watch what they say and do, a great opportunity to learn and improve and to validate of what you are doing is right.
- Reflect and learn through experience
- Always look for something new to improve and be better
- Learn from your heroes

I really hope that you have enjoyed reading this book as I share my insights and my story to date. I hope that it has

Chapter 14: Continue to Develop Yourself

had an influence on you and that it has inspired you to develop the intelligent young footballer.

My closing message for you...

Continue to enjoy, embrace and love this beautiful game and appreciate that you have one of life's privileges... to be able to grow, influence, inspire and develop the intelligent young footballer.

All the best,
Mike